Advance Praise For
(TRANS)NATIONAL TSINA/OYS

"This book is a travelogue to places and spaces of knowing the self in culture; crossing borders to different but familiar locations, and (re)discovering the socializing practices that shape culture and identity. Hao introduces us to complex ways of revisiting notions of intersectionality not just through the complex meeting places of oppressions in social contexts, but through the importance of *a diasporic transnational hybridity*. He eschews the notion of hybridity as just a mixture of discrete cultures, but the complex co-informing aspects of ethnicity, nationality, class, and the politics of place that shape a sense of self in relation to common origins and the performative variations of identity that are held in contradistinction to those shared roots. Using diverse and interlocking ethnographic and qualitative methodologies, *(Trans)national Tsina/oys: Hybrid Performances of Chinese and Filipina/o Identities* asks the reader to engage at the intersections, the hyphens, and the parenthetical constructions of hybridity that make the subjects of the study, including himself, both/and always searching for homeplace in communities of recognized co-informing identities that are at once the same and not the same."
— *Bryant Keith Alexander, Ph.D., Dean and Professor, College of Communication and Fine Arts, Loyola Marymount University*

"*(Trans)national Tsina/oys: Hybrid Performances of Chinese and Filipina/o Identities* stands as an exemplar of critical intercultural communication studies and the deep-level insights that it provides as a field to uncover the intricately woven layers of cultural identity, performativity, belonging, and the cultural politics that constitute 'home.' Dr. Hao's book also highlights the key role that critical intercultural communication studies plays in unpacking the complex of diasporas in terms of (but not limited to) their identity dynamics, the power effects in claiming/remembering/clarifying one's identity in relation to a 'home' (of memory, of place, of relational cultural space), and the thorny assemblage of meaning around 'belonging.'"
— *Rona Tamiko Halualani, Ph.D., Professor of Intercultural Communication, Department of Communication Studies, San Jose State University*

(TRANS)NATIONAL TSINA/OYS

Thomas K. Nakayama and Bernadette Marie Calafell,

GENERAL EDITOR

vol. 17

Richie Neil Hao

(TRANS)NATIONAL TSINA/OYS

Hybrid Performances of Chinese and Filipina/o Identities

PETER LANG
Lausanne • Berlin • Bruxelles • Chennai • New York • Oxford

Library of Congress Cataloging-in-Publication Control Number: 2022053942

Bibliographic information published by the Deutsche Nationalbibliothek.
The German National Library lists this publication in the German
National Bibliography; detailed bibliographic data is available
on the Internet at http://dnb.d-nb.de.

Cover design by Peter Lang Group AG

ISBN 9781433186622 (paperback)
ISBN 9781433186639 (ebook)
ISBN 9781433186646 (epub)
DOI 10.3726/ b20321

© 2023 Peter Lang Group AG, Lausanne
Published by Peter Lang Publishing Inc., New York, USA
info@peterlang.com - www.peterlang.com

All rights reserved.
All parts of this publication are protected by copyright.
Any utilization outside the strict limits of the copyright law, without the permission of the publisher, is forbidden and liable to prosecution.
This applies in particular to reproductions, translations, microfilming, and storage and processing in electronic retrieval systems.

This publication has been peer reviewed.

To Anh and Hieubert

CONTENTS

Acknowledgments ix
List of Abbreviations xi

Rediscovering Tsina/oy Identity: A Critical Intercultural Performance   1

Documenting Tsina/oy Voices: Identities and Representation in (Trans)national Spaces   25

Performing Tsina/oyness: (E)merging Chinese and Filipina/o Identities   47

Becoming Tsinoy American: (Trans)national Identity and Citizenship   71

Virtually Tsina/oy: Performing Hybridity Online   91

Generational Tsina/oys: (Auto)ethnographic Reflections and Future Directions   111

Index   129

ACKNOWLEDGMENTS

Writing this book has been a long journey, and there are so many people who have contributed to the completion of this project. First and foremost, I am thankful for the love and support of Anh Huynh and Hieubert Hao. Both have been incredibly patient and encouraging throughout the process of writing this book. I am and will always be grateful to my parents (Jose Andres and Salome Hao) and my siblings (Beanne, Mark, Ryan, and Stephanie), all of whom have taught me everything about my Tsinoy identity. My great appreciation goes to *a-má* and Susan Hao for their generosity and kindness. Thanks also to Crispin and Betty Hao, my extended families, and my in-laws for their continued support.

My book would not have come to fruition without the research grant I received from the University of Denver's Center for Multicultural Excellence that made it possible for me to conduct ethnographic interviews in the Philippines. In addition to Susan Hao, Cheryl Hao deserves many thanks for helping me with recruitment of Tsina/oy participants. Of course, all my Tsina/oy participants, the wonderful staff at Bahay Tsinoy, and Teresita Ang See's influential scholarship on Tsina/oys are the reasons I have a book to write. Thank you so much! My appreciation also goes to Stephanie Hao, who designed my book's cover.

A big thank you to editors and reviewers. I want to thank Bernadette Marie Calafell and Thomas K. Nakayama for including my book in the Critical Intercultural Communication Studies Series. I am especially grateful for their belief in my project from the very beginning. A big shout-out to Peter Lang's editorial team, especially Niall Kennedy and Joshua Charles, and Production Editor Naviya Palani. Thanks to my writing coaches who provided an extra set of eyes to improve the book's contents: Bryant Keith Alexander, Shinsuke Eguchi, Greg Langner, and Dawn Marie McIntosh.

Grateful acknowledgment is made to the following for permission to reproduce copyrighted material:

"Critical Intercultural Performance Framework: Transnational Hybridity as Performance of Reentries," R. N. Hao, *Journal of Intercultural Communication Research*, copyright © 2020 World Communication Association reprinted by permission of Taylor & Francis Ltd, http://www.tandfonline.com on behalf of World Communication Association.

"Cultural Reentry: A Critical Review of Intercultural Communication Research," R. N. Hao, in N. Bardhan and M. O. Orbe (Eds.), *Identity Research and Communication: Intercultural Reflections and Future Directions*, Lexington Books. 2012 All Rights Reserved.

"Virtually Tsina/oy: Performing and Negotiating Diasporic Hybridity Online," by R. N. Hao, 2013, *Qualitative Communication Research*, 2, pp. 159–181. Copyright 2013 by The Regents of the University of California (University of California Press). Reprinted with permission.

I am also deeply indebted to Bryant Keith Alexander and John T. Warren's mentorship; both have had tremendous impact on my scholarship and pedagogy. Along with John T. Warren, thanks to Nilanjana Bardhan, Craig Engstrom, Jonathan Gray, Rachel Hastings, Kathy Hytten, Cheryl Nicholas, and Ronald Pelias for reviewing an earlier version of Chapter Five, "Virtually Tsina/oy: Performing Hybridity Online." Their feedback at the time made a huge difference to get me where I am today to publish this book. Finally, I want to thank Robin Boylorn, Rona Tamiko Halualani, Judith Hamera, and Mark Orbe for their (auto)ethnographic scholarly inspiration and collaboration that helped shape the trajectory of this book!

LIST OF ABBREVIATIONS

Abbreviation	Meaning
CIP	Critical Intercultural Performance
FFCCCII	Federation of Filipino-Chinese Chambers of Commerce and Industry, Inc.
TSA	Transportation Security Administration
USCIS	United States Citizenship and Immigration Services

REDISCOVERING TSINA/OY IDENTITY: A CRITICAL INTERCULTURAL PERFORMANCE

November 29, 2010. I arrive at Denver International Airport and approach one of the airline's self-serve electronic ticket kiosks to print my three boarding passes (from Denver to Los Angeles, Los Angeles to Tokyo, and Tokyo to Manila). What was normally a routine of being able to print my boarding pass(es) when flying domestically in the United States, this time something unusual flashes on the computer screen: "Please see the attendant to process your request." I follow the directions on the screen. I step into the counter closest to me and mention to the attendant that the self-serve ticketing couldn't process my request. She asks me where I'm heading. "Manila," I say to her. In that moment, I just realized that I'm not only visiting Manila, but I'm returning home for the first time in 17 years. As I take my seat on the plane and start pondering about my travel to Los Angeles and Tokyo, before arriving to my final destination in Manila, I think about what these places are to me. When the plane arrives in Los Angeles, I feel (un)easiness as it reminds me of my family who lives in the suburbs about 45 miles away. In Los Angeles I have to go through another security screening that will take me to the international terminal for my flight to Tokyo. As I embark on a 16-hour flight, I experience international travel for the first time since my family and I left Manila for Los Angeles when I was 13 years old.

After three connecting flights, the plane descends to the ground of Ninoy Aquino International Airport in Manila, Philippines. As I walk out of the plane to the gate area, anxiety and excitement simultaneously fuel my body. I cannot help but notice the Christmas decorations and lights along the way, which are very telling of the holiday season. After locating my luggage, I wait patiently outside of the airport terminal swarmed by many Filipina/os who, like me, are eager to be picked up. Hearing Tagalog or Taglish (a combination of Tagalog and English) spoken all around me is familiar. Almost another hour has passed at roughly 10:45 p.m., I suddenly hear someone calling my name in the midst of honking cars driving past me. I turn to my left, and I see a blurred face from a distance waving and continuing to yell my name. A tall, slender woman comes closer, and as soon as I recognize my aunt I hurriedly pick up my carry-on bag right next to me, put it on top of my suitcase, and move all the luggage towards a parked van on the curbside. As soon as I approach my aunt, she welcomes me warmly in Hokkien, a local Chinese language we both speak, while simultaneously directing me where to put my luggage in the van.

As the van departs the crowded and heavily trafficked airport, my aunt, whom I have not seen in almost two decades, engages in a small talk to see how I have been all these years. Driving by the city with several well-lit tall buildings with Christmas lights and *parols* (star-shaped Christmas lanterns) hung around several houses and businesses, my aunt asks me if I think things have changed since I lived in Manila. While observing quietly through the van's window, I do not hesitate to point out to my aunt that I did not see many tall skylines and expansive shopping malls that populate the city as a child, but crowded streets remain unchanged.

Shortly past midnight, we arrive at my 95-year-old grandmother and aunt's apartment in Binondo, a Chinatown neighborhood of Manila. I look at the towering building right in front of me before entering the glass doors where I see the security guard, who smiles at my aunt upon seeing her, opens the metal gated door instantly. We go into the elevator and arrive on the eleventh floor. Upon turning left from the elevator and another right at the end of the hallway, I immediately recognize where the apartment is located. My aunt and I enter the apartment, which is mostly dark except for the light in the living room. Since it is past midnight, my aunt directs me to my grandmother, who is asleep in her bedroom, to quickly say hello. Although woken up suddenly, my grandmother is extremely happy to see me. Without keeping her up for more than five minutes, I exit the bedroom and take a seat on the couch in the living room trying to soak everything in. As a kid, I remember frequenting the apartment with my parents and siblings during my grandmother's birthdays, Lunar New Years, Mid-Autumn (Mooncake) Festivals, and other family gatherings. Even though my family and I occasionally celebrate these cultural traditions to some extent in the United States, being in Manila, particularly in my grandmother's apartment, serves as a bridge that reminds me of a locational practice that culture exists performatively of what it means to be Tsinoy. "Tsinoy" refers to Chinese Filipino or Filipino with Chinese ancestry (See, 2016). It is a combination of "Tsino" (Chinese) and "Pinoy" (colloquial for Filipino), which results in the hybrid identity of "Tsinoy" (Yap, 2018).[i]

Based on my and other Tsina/oys' experiences, my goal in this book is to examine and analyze Tsina/oy identity as performance of (trans)national hybridity in physical and online contexts. To do that, I start this opening chapter with an overview of how Tsina/oy identity has changed historically, politically, and socially. Second, I discuss why it is appropriate to consider Tsina/oys as (trans)national hybrids. Third, I introduce Critical Intercultural Performance (CIP) as a framework to emphasize intersectionality and reflexivity as a (trans)national Tsinoy researcher. I end with a preview of the book's remaining chapters.

Tsina/oys: Performing Chinese and Filipina/o Identities

Like many ethnic Chinese around the world, the Chinese in the Philippines have complex historical, social, and political identities. Ethnic Chinese are

> people with a measurable degree of Chinese parentage, have undergone a minimum Chinese-language education, can understand and speak a bare minimum of Chinese dialect, still have close contacts with the Chinese community, and have retained some Chinese customs and traditions, enough to consider themselves and be considered by others as Chinese. (See, 1997b, p. 42)

Most Chinese in the Philippines—Tsina/oys—can trace their roots to Fujian and Guangdong provinces in southern China. According to See (1997a), "Harsh economic and political conditions in China" resulted in the Chinese immigrating to the Philippines (p. 78). Tsina/oys are heterogenous as a cultural group. Some have 100% Chinese blood, while others are mestiza/os with 50% or 25% Chinese blood, or of Chinese descent but are several generations removed (See, 1997a). In fact, about 85% of Tsina/oys were born and raised as second, third, and fourth generation in the Philippines (See, 1997b).

The vast majority of Tsina/oys today are Filipina/o citizens who reside in the Metro Manila area (See, 1997b), such as Binondo (Manila's Chinatown) and surrounding cities like Quezon City (Gonzales, 2016). Unlike ethnic Chinese in other parts of Asia, Tsina/oys are a minority with approximately 1.2 million of the Philippines' population (See, 2016), which would be considered one of the smallest Chinese ethnic groups in Southeast Asia (Sy, 2015). The small number of ethnic Chinese in the Philippines can be attributed to the country's lengthy past as Spanish and U.S. colonies (See, 2004).

Colonial Pasts and Transnational Movements

The Chinese first set foot in the Philippines as traders during the Sung Period (960–1279) (Wickberg, 1965). The growing presence of the Chinese in the Philippines became evident even before the Spanish settled in the Philippines (See, 2004). The Spaniards referred to the Chinese as "Sangleys" (frequent visitors) for their trading relationship during the Spanish colonization (1521–1898) (Uytanlet, 2016). The Philippine economy was still in early developmental stages when the Chinese came to fill in the gaps as merchants during the Spanish colonial rule (See, 1997a). Because the Chinese were not allowed to own land, they could not work in agriculture. Lack of citizenship also prevented the Chinese from entering other professions, so it made sense to start their businesses, even though their previous living experiences in rural China did not prepare them to do so. Despite rampant discrimination against the Chinese, their population continued to increase in the early 1600s that threatened the Spaniards, resulting in Chinese persecution and massacre especially those who resisted to become Christians during 1603–1820 (Tan, 1972).

A new wave of Chinese immigrants arrived in the Philippines in the 1830s (Wickberg, 1965). From the 1860s until 1898, many Chinese primarily worked as traders, fishers, bakers, and butchers (Doeppers, 1986), while other Chinese immigrants, especially in Manila, worked in restaurant and shoemaking businesses (Chu, 2010). However, temporary growth in Chinese immigration was halted due to the implementation of the Chinese Exclusion Act to the U.S.-colonized Philippines in 1902, which "allowed the entry only of Chinese merchants and their immediate families into the country" (See, 2004, p. 32). Continued discrimination forced many Chinese to live in enclaves like Binondo that limited their economic opportunities (Gonzales, 2017).

Several decades later, President Ferdinand Marcos signed the Letter of Instruction 270 in 1975 that granted mass naturalization of the Chinese (Tan, 1988). As a result, most Chinese eventually became Filipina/o citizens, which provided opportunities for them to enter different professions in law, medicine, architecture, engineering, and the arts (Hau, 2005). Different professional opportunities afforded many Tsina/oys to enter the middle class and play a significant role in various aspects of the Philippine economy (Chua, 2003), such as in agriculture, banking, finance, and real estate (Rivera & Koike, 1995). It is important to note, however, that there are Filipina/os who own some of the biggest companies in the Philippines (Cariño, 2001) and Tsina/oys who are extremely poor (See, 1997a). Poverty among Tsina/oys is usually unheard of "because in most circumstances, they have assimilated into Philippine society and often, their Filipino neighbors are not even aware of the families being Chinese" (p. 31). Even though many Tsina/oys have successfully acculturated (and assimilated) to the Filipina/o culture, they continue to embody their Chinese identity as part of their hybridity.

Becoming Tsina/oys: Possibilities and Challenges

Because their ancestry can be traced to Fujian and Guangdong provinces in China, most first-generation Chinese immigrants spoke Hokkien (a southern Chinese language) socially and economically (Klöter, 2011). However, colonial pasts affected linguistic practices among the Chinese in the Philippines. The arrival of the Spaniards and U.S. Americans mandated the use of Spanish and English, respectively, in the Philippines. Between 1935 and 1946 Spanish remained the "language of law" (Thompson, 2003, p. 27), while English was used in the courts and instruction (Gonzalez, 2004). Yet, an exception was made for the Chinese to establish Chinese schools that had English, Hokkien (or Cantonese), and/or Mandarin language instruction (Chu, 2010; Gonzales, 2017). English ultimately served as the language of business, while Hokkien functioned as the primary language in the Chinese community. Establishing Chinese schools was one of the many efforts for Tsina/oys to maintain their Chinese language and culture (See, 1997a). To this day, there are about 130 Chinese Filipina/o schools in the Philippines, and almost half are in Metro Manila (Sy, 2015).

When the U.S. occupation was ending, Philippine President Manuel L. Quezon named Spanish-influenced Tagalog as the national language in 1937 (Thompson, 2003). Tagalog and English subsequently became co-dominant languages, which evolved into a hybridized language called "Taglish" (Bautista, 2004). Even though many Chinese in the Philippines across different generations speak Hokkien, those who were local born tend to speak Tagalog or a Filipina/o dialect and English as their primary languages (See, 1997b). It is also not uncommon for Tsina/oys to speak Mandarin with a variety of fluency (See, 1997a).

Aside from performing their Chinese and Filipina/o identities through languages they speak, Tsina/oys continue to engage in (trans)national cultural and religious practices. Many Tsina/oys have long celebrated the Mid-Autumn (Mooncake) Festival and Lunar New Year as part of their Chinese identity for generations (Yu, 2000). In addition, because of their Chinese identity and the effects of Spanish and U.S. colonization, Tsina/oys tend to engage in hybridized religious practices. In fact, most Tsina/oys are Christians, but "a growing number of them subscribe to another religion or a religious practice that is a mixture of Christianity, Buddhism, Taoism, and what can be ascribed as folk or traditional religion" (See, 2004, pp. 181–182), which explains why it is not unusual to see both churches and temples surrounding the cities that Tsina/oys inhabit (Guéguen, 2010).

The rich historical, political, and cultural transitions and tensions that Tsina/oys faced have undoubtedly shaped their Chinese and Filipina/o identities today. See (1997a) states the following:

> They [Philippine Chinese] have little or no first-hand experience of China, and they consider the Philippines as their one and only home. The grant[ing] of Filipino citizenship lifted the stumbling block that barred them from totally committing themselves to Philippine society and identifying themselves politically as Filipinos. Yet, before mass naturalization and full integration happened, giving rise to a new identity and orientation, many young Chinese went through the agonizing experience of being marginal people—not belonging to Philippine society and yet not fully identifying themselves with the Chinese community. (pp. 6–7)

Many Tsina/oys feel the in-betweenness of negotiating Chinese and Filipina/o identities. As an effort to integrate and advocate for the Chinese in Philippine society, *Kaisa* (also known as *Kaisa para sa Kaunlaran*, which means "Unity in Progress") was established in 1987 (Cariño, 1988). In 1992 *Kaisa* coined the term, "Tsinoy," to distinguish local born Chinese Filipina/os from new or recent immigrants from China (Uytanlet, 2016). Navigating both Chinese and Filipina/o cultures, Tsina/oys have experienced many historical, social, and political shifts affecting their identities for centuries, so it is appropriate for their bodies to be considered (trans)national hybrids.

Tsina/oys as (Trans)national Hybridity

November 30, 2010. As a (trans)national Tsinoy from the United States, it is surreal to return to Manila after all these years. I sit silently in my grandmother's living room. I look around my surroundings, and much has remained the same except for the repositioning of the couch and TV stand to the opposite side of the wall. The living room flows seamlessly to the open dining area where many of the family gatherings took place to catch up with relatives while eating a mixture of Chinese and Filipina/o foods to celebrate special occasions. Because of the limited seating in the dining area, I, as a kid, sat at the "kiddie table" in the living room. Although the "kiddie table" may seem insignificant, it reminds me of my childhood where my cousins and I learned about different Chinese and Filipina/o traditions that ultimately shaped our hybrid identity as future generations of Tsina/oys.

Because many Tsina/oys today are at least a few generations removed from their Chinese ancestors and only know the Philippines as their home (See, 1997a), diaspora does not always accurately define their experiences. According to Clifford (1994), diasporas connect multiple communities (e.g., ethnic, overseas, immigrant, refugee, expatriate, guest-worker, exiled, etc.) of a dispersed population. Diasporas can also be a result of

> war or ethnic conflict, slavery, indentured labor, natural disasters, the postcolonial "brain-drain" of professionals to the lands of former colonizers and the global North, and more recently, the movement of skilled and unskilled migrant labor in the global circuits of decentered capitalism. (Bardhan, 2011, p. 42)

Due to voluntary and involuntary migration, diaspora tends to focus on ethnicity, "which privileges the point of 'origin' in constructing identity and solidarity" (Anthias, 1998, p. 558). In essence, as Besserer (2018) notes, "The concept of 'diaspora' has been used by states to recognize as nationals those people who can be found outside its national borders" (p. 122), which is why diasporic individuals experience tension between home and host cultures (Bardhan, 2011; Drzewiecka, 2002; Shi, 2005; Vertovec, 1997) who long for belonging or a return to the original homeland (Anderson, 1998; Appadurai, 1990; Clifford, 1994; Safran, 1991; Tölölyan, 1996).

Unfortunately, "in much of the literature [on diaspora] there is a presumed relationship between the diasporic community and the land that they left and to which the possibility of return always subsists..., but this presumed link between the diasporic community and the motherland is easily questioned"

(Gajjala, 2004, pp. 64–65). With that in mind, diasporic experiences are often linked with adaptation processes that constitute these predictive steps: "1) entry into and adjustment in a new culture and 2) re-entry back into the original culture" (Halualani, 2008, p. 6). There is an assumption with diaspora that "cultural meanings and identities remain fixed in particular spaces: the original homeland as more traditional and authentic and the new home-space as 'modern'" (pp. 6–7).

In addition to much of diaspora literature's focus on collective individuals' desire to return home, another area of critique is that it does not necessarily address intersectional identities (Anthias, 1998; Brah, 1996; hooks, 1981). As a result, "diaspora tends to homogenise the population" in question (Anthias, 1998, p. 564). To the contrary, Anthias (1998) emphasizes that "movements of population may have taken place at different historical periods and for different reasons, and different countries of destination provided different social conditions, opportunities and exclusions" (p. 564). I turn to transnationalism because many Tsina/oy bodies cannot accurately be represented simply as diasporic in nature, especially those who were born and raised in the Philippines.

Transnationalism as a concept also breaks away from "national" studies of diaspora (Besserer, 2018; Gilroy, 1993) to reinforce "fluid social spaces that are constantly reworked" in between societies (Levitt & Jaworsky, 2007, p. 131). Besserer (2018) notes that transnationalism examines "how one might imagine other worlds where the construction of citizenship, security and governance can be thought without resorting to the model of nationalism" (p. 121). Therefore, transnationalism challenges nationhood and citizenship (Basch et al., 1995) by making connections between multiple cultures that results in the creation of new categories (Bardhan, 2011; Drzewiecka, 2002; Nurse, 1999) and borderland identities (Alexander, 2006; Anzaldúa, 1999; Aparicio, 2004; Calafell, 2005; Cheng, 2008; Còrdoba, 2005). Transnationalism also communicates "hybridity continuum" that emphasizes the intersectionality of race, gender, and class (Levitt & Jaworsky, 2007, p. 139), which is critical in understanding the complexity and diversity of hybrid identities.

More importantly, transnationalism takes into account the evolving relationship between state and nation (Tyrrell, 2001) and acknowledges diasporic experiences during pre-national and contemporary times (Besserer, 2018). In essence, transnationalism makes it possible to focus on inter-domestic interactions. Situating transnationalism in local contexts is especially helpful in articulating how Tsina/oys perform their Chinese and Filipina/o identities relative to where they are located physically and virtually. By using transnationalism, I argue that cultural identities are localized as practiced performances of cultural knowing through language, customs, and rituals that signal communal connections that are recognizable by others. In other words, performing cultural identities, such as Tsina/oy identity, is influenced by social actors who engage in performance and performative events that communicate familiar experiences (Alexander et al., 2005). Therefore, I argue that transnational is an appropriate term to describe Tsina/oys across generations who embody Chinese and Filipina/o identities in a variety of ways.

However, I must caution that transnationalism's "primary concern still rests on the transgression of and exchange beyond national borders" (Greiner & Sakdapolrak, 2013, p. 374). Rather than constructing all Tsina/oys as perpetual members of the Chinese diaspora who move across national borders, I specifically use "(trans)national" to recognize multiple realities (the local and the global) and distinguish that not all Tsina/oys are mobile, migrants, cross borders, or have cultural ties with China or other countries. Using (trans)national to describe Tsina/oys also prompts us to acknowledge that many of them were born and raised in the Philippines, have always lived in the Philippines, and constitute Tsina/oyness as part of their Filipina/o national identity. In fact, it has always been paramount for Tsina/oys to exemplify their Filipina/o national identity in order to fit into the Philippine society (See, 1997a). After all, due to hybridity, cultural "transformations are tied to the politics of belonging and citizenship" (Levitt & Jaworsky, 2007, p. 140). As Tsina/oys constantly negotiate their Chinese and Filipina/o identities, it is crucial to consider hybridity when discussing multiple identities in (trans)national contexts. Even though there are many ways to conceptualize hybridity, I will primarily focus on how hybridity both communicates fluid identities in (trans)national spaces and experiences multiple tensions.

Hybridity as Fluid Identities

November 30, 2010. While in my grandmother's living room, I can't help but ponder about the reality of being in Manila. It took me almost two decades to finally return home. I was a kid the last time I was in this apartment, let alone in the country of my birth. Standing in front of my grandmother's living room window, I can see a bird's eye view of the well-lit city and hear the traffic noise in the background. Ironically, the bright lights and honking sound do not disturb me even past the midnight hour; they complement the hustle and bustle of Manila's Chinatown neighborhood, which remind me of home and my hybrid Tsinoy identity.

As "relational subjectivity," hybridity engages in "both conscious and unconscious performances of (hybrid) selves" as a communicative process (Young, 2009, p. 159) in a "space where bodies and identity resist stable categories, and [where] meaning is ambivalent, contradictory, and historically shifting" (Molina Guzmán & Valdivia, 2004, p. 214). As such, hybridity is ambiguous, dynamic, unstable, and blends cultures and provides opportunities for development of new structures, perspectives, and spaces (e.g., Anzaldúa, 1999; Bakhtin, 1981; Bhabha, 1994; Calafell, 2004; García Canclini, 1995; Gilroy, 1993; Hall, 1996; Halualani, 2008; Hao, 2012; Kraidy, 2005; Naficy, 1993; Turner, 1969).

Hybridity also allows for ongoing cultural experiences as "a legitimate process" (Pascual, 2004, pp. 288–289) to find alternatives to resist the dominant power (Alexander, 2006; Eguchi, 2014; Halualani, 2008; Hegde, 2002; hooks, 1990) and dismantle the notion of a unitary identity (Alexander, 2004; Anthias, 2001; Bhabha, 1994; Calafell, 2007; Halualani, 2008; Hao, 2013). Because in "its preoccupation with the control, classification, and surveillance of its subjects, the nation-state has often created, revitalized, or fractured ethnic identities that were previously fluid, negotiable, or nascent" (Appadurai, 1996, p. 162). Therefore, "we need to think ourselves beyond the nation" (p. 158). With borders being redefined politically and economically, "the borders of the 'nation' as both 'a community of strangers' (Us), juxtaposed to a 'strange community' (Others), also become re-defined" (Anthias, 2001, p. 635, emphasis in original). In fact, hybrid individuals, especially those who are migrants, do not simply search for their ethnic origins, but rather they negotiate their transnational identities in a new cultural space (Hall, 1996). Perhaps that is why Gómez-Peña (1996) calls cultural hybrids as "Fourth World" people because they resist the "Third World/First World dichotomy" for living in a space that has little room for "static identities, fixed nationalities, 'pure' languages, or sacred cultural traditions" (p. 7). To that end, hybridity is characterized as a subversion of political and cultural domination, which moves away from singularities of race, gender, generation, sexual orientation, institutional location, and geographical locale where new signs of identity and innovative sites of contestation and collaboration are created in in-between spaces (Bhabha, 1994).

Due to globalization, transnational identities continue to evolve and change in various physical and online spaces where "subjectivities are constructed based on access to and ability to perform the cultural practices and norms of a given locale, giving rise to hybrid cultural forms and identities" (Gordon, 2016, p. 231). Globalization also provides images of culture that are diverse, non-coherent, complex, interactive, dynamic, and political (Alexander, 2006; Anzaldúa, 1999; Featherstone, 1995; Pascual, 2004), which makes transnationalism especially relevant to understanding hybrid identities. As Kraidy (2005) asserts, "Since hybridity involves the fusion of two hitherto relatively distinct forms, styles, or identities, cross-cultural contact, which often occurs across national borders as well as across cultural boundaries, is a requisite for hybridity" (p. 5). Hybridity's ability to reconstruct identities in transnational spaces makes it possible for such identities to continue to evolve and change over time (Anthias, 2001).

Hybridity and Multiple Tensions

While hybridity provides opportunities for performance of different identities, it can also pose multiple tensions (Alexander, 2006; Joseph, 1999; Yep, 2002) due to third space positionalities (Bhabha, 1994). Third space, or in-between, positionalities can be understood as "the space at the intersection of structure (as social position/social effects) and agency (as social positioning/meaning and practice)" (Anthias, 2001, p. 635). Young (2009) further notes,

> Hybrid identity is considered indefinable, embodying multiple positionalities that emerge in moments of change. Such identities are continuously being made and remade through social interactions...[where] one may choose to perform one identity in one specific setting, another identity in another setting, or both simultaneously. (p. 141)

Because hybridity constantly challenges what it means to be included and excluded, Anthias (2001) calls for "translocational positionality" to acknowledge the significance of context to address the complexity and contradictory nature of positionalities by engaging in the intersectionality of race, ethnicity, nationality, gender, and class within hybridity (p. 634). As an example, Anzaldúa (1999) communicates about the struggles she faced as multicultural and multilingual in different contexts, and how that felt like battling an inner war:

> Cradled in one culture, sandwiched between two cultures, straddling in all three cultures and their value systems, *la mestiza* undergoes a struggle of flesh, a struggle of borders, an inner war. Like all people, we perceive the version of reality that our culture communicates. Like others having or living in more than one culture, we get multiple, often opposing messages. (p. 378)

Since hybridity is "full of discontinuities and ruptures" (Anthias, 2001, p. 626), fractured and conflicted (Shome, 1996), multiple tensions can occur for people who are multicultural. After all, hybridity engages in what Bhabha (1994) calls "mimicry—the almost but not quite—" construction of hybrid individuals who cannot seem to fit in as part of their respective cultural groups (p. 91). For instance, immigrants' "intercultural identity" engages in "balancing acts between two cultures—sustaining the traditions and cultural practices of their country of origin while simultaneously adopting foreign customs in an attempt to survive in their 'new' country" (Young, 2009, p. 142). Regardless of the cultural performances they engage in, immigrants often find it difficult to embody specific expectations of how to look, sound, and act in order to be accepted as in-group members.

Multiple tensions can also emerge as a result of "how hegemonic structures operate in a variety of contexts to construct different hybridities" (Kraidy, 2002, p. 334). Within hybridity, hierarchization can materialize to highlight "a hierarchy of places (and specification of which types of individuals may or may not fill them) within what may be called an ethnic or racialized space" (Anthias, 2001, pp. 634–635). Shugart (2007) warns, "Certainly, hybridity also constitutes a threat, but its very instability renders it an ideal vehicle for all manner of representations that can be marshaled in various ways to negotiate potential ruptures to a discourse of whiteness" (p. 121). Hybridity, therefore, can be performed as "a consequence of a whimsical yet unwieldy and ultimately unfeasible collision rather than conflation or fusion of cultures, thereby securing and reinforcing the borders of whiteness" (p. 121). Additionally, hybridities can function as *practices of hegemony* that "illuminate the slippery and interstitial workings of power in transnational contexts" (Kraidy, 2002, p. 335, emphasis in original). Considering hybridity in (trans)national contexts, it is especially important to emphasize intersectionality and reflexivity to examine diverse Tsina/oy voices and experiences.

Critical Intercultural Performance: Identities, Intersectionality, and Reflexivity

November 30, 2010. I enter a bedroom that my aunt had prepared for my three-week stay. I listen to the murmur of the air conditioner while observing my new environment. I unpack my suitcases slowly and place them neatly against the wall. I pick up and unzip my backpack to make sure my permanent residency card and passport are placed in the same pocket. After peeking through these documents, I begin to think about the different privileges I have as a documented (trans)national hybrid whose body is legitimized to cross borders. As a college educated, middle class, and documented permanent resident of the United States, I recognize that my privileged body affords me to travel between the United States and Philippines with less restrictions than other people. Acknowledging my privileges as a (trans)national researcher and how they influence my understanding of Tsina/oy identity prompts me to think about intersectionality and reflexivity, which is why I call for Critical Intercultural Performance (CIP) (Hao, 2020).

The critical turn in intercultural communication emphasizes how historical, social, and political contexts function as power in shaping identities (e.g., Alexander et al., 2014; Collier et al., 2001; Hall, 1992; Halualani & Nakayama, 2010; Leeds-Hurwitz, 1990; Moon, 1996; Ono, 1998; Warren, 2008), which reinforces that culture is "a site of struggle where various communication meanings are constructed" (Martin & Nakayama, 1999, p. 8). Halualani et al. (2009) also stress, "History as context plays a major role in constituting intercultural interactions and reproducing power relations that are embedded in historical and contested struggles over issues of belonging and ethnic rights" (p. 22). Therefore, critical intercultural communication scholars view culture "as a politicized system of signification, the semiotic terrain of an ideological struggle of vested interests where cultural terms for negotiation of identities are deployed, appropriated, and contested" (p. 23).

Even though critical intercultural communication focuses on power and its effects on cultural identities, Calafell (2014) advocates for performance to locate the body as a way of knowing:

> Performance works from the ground up as it situates us in the everyday. Through this it works to reconfigure relations of power. It works against dominant conceptions of knowledge by locating itself in and theorizing through the body. It offers us a critical interpretive tool and lens. (p. 116)

Working through the body as a form of knowledge, performance studies is committed to "create performances that network and interrogate relationships between, and conventions of, performance and/as representation" (Madison & Hamera, 2006, p. xxii). Compared to traditional rhetorical methods, performance studies offers "more complex approaches to embodiment, resistance, and cultural nuances—particularly when examining work by historically marginalized groups" (Calafell, 2014, p. 115). Performance allows possibilities to demonstrate "embodied experience grounded in historical process, contingency, and ideology" (Conquergood, 1991, p. 187), especially for identities in borderlands (Alexander, 2004; Anzaldúa, 1999; Calafell, 2007; Rosaldo, 1989). Situating performance in (trans)national spaces by referencing de Certeau (1984), Madison and Hamera (2006) argue that "performance becomes the enactment and evidence of stories that literally and figuratively bleed across the borders" (p. xx).

Inspired by Madison and Hamera's (2006) work, I conceptualize hybridity—specifically, Tsina/oy identity—as embodiment of cultural identities in (trans)national spaces (Hao, 2020). Drawing from my own (trans)national experiences and literature in critical intercultural communication and performance studies, I introduce CIP to mark my positionality as a Tsinoy researcher who makes a connection between the framework's two tenets: intersectionality and reflexivity.

(Trans)national Hybrid Intersectionality

CIP's first tenet addresses intersectionality to understand the complexity of (trans)national hybridity (Hao, 2020). With Crenshaw's (1989, 1991) introduction of the concept of intersectionality, Collins's (1990) matrix of domination has also been instrumental in intersectionality research. Since then, many critical intercultural communication scholars (e.g., Alexander, 2006; Chrifi Alaoui & Calafell, 2016; Calafell et al., 2020; Eguchi, 2014; Johnson & LeMaster, 2020; McIntosh & Hobson, 2013; Yep, 2016) have extended Crenshaw and Collins's research on intersectionality. As an example, Yep (2016) defines intersectionality as the following: "Intersectionality refers to how race, class, gender, sexuality, the body, and nation, among other vectors of difference, come together simultaneously to produce social identities and experiences in the social world, from privilege to oppression" (p. 86). These multiple and intersectional identities are arbitrary, contested, and contextual (Alexander, 2006; Moreman, 2008). To that end, I support Moon's (1996) call for an examination of our multiple and intersectional identities and how our positionality, which is informed within social structures, "affects and/or is constructed in intercultural interactions" (p. 76).

A major critique of contemporary approaches to intersectionality, especially from the perspective of women and queer of color feminisms, is that they do not necessarily address nationality and citizenship (Chrifi Alaoui & Calafell, 2016), politics (Calafell et al., 2020), and the role of space in identity construction

(Yep, 2016). Inspired by my own experience traveling transnationally and recent work on intersectionality (e.g., Alexander, 2017; Calafell et al., 2020; Chrifi Alaoui & Calafell, 2016; Eguchi, 2011; Ghabra & Calafell, 2018; McIntosh & Hobson, 2013; Yep, 2016), I argue that it is critical to include (un)documented bodies as another layer of intersectionality (Hao, 2020). Documentation, such as passport, permanent residency card, travel/student/work visas, among others, has tremendous implications on how (trans)national hybrid bodies are read and their ability to cross (trans)national borders. Because (trans)national hybrids could be citizens of different countries, could identify with multiple nationalities, or may lack documentation to recognize their national identity, (un)documented bodies have different sets of challenges and privileges. In particular, brown and black bodies holding a passport from a developing nation while traveling would have a different experience from someone who is carrying a U.S. passport, which comes with different privileges, such as not having to attain a travel visa in several countries. However, even with proper documentation, brown and black bodies from the United States often experience racial profiling or discrimination when traveling (trans)nationally, which is why reflexivity is another important consideration for CIP.

(Trans)national Hybrid Reflexivity

CIP's second tenet provides an understanding of the role of power in cultural identity construction through (trans)national hybrid reflexivity. It is imperative for us to ask critical questions of how power shapes our culture: "Who ultimately has the power/privilege/right to define and reproduce 'culture'? Who benefits from the creation of 'culture'?" (Halualani, 1998, p. 267). Halualani (2000) proposes "structural-cultural projects" when looking at culture by connecting the structural to everyday interactions, especially when engaging in reflexivity. Reflexivity is the interrogation of the self, which locates the authoring self as a teacher or researcher to understand what the subject becomes and who the subject authors in response (Warren & Fassett, 2002). Chen and Lin (2016) add, "The study of cultural identities should encourage reflexive understandings of both one's own and others' identities in manners that promote productive intercultural encounters, interactions, and relationships" (Conclusions section, para. 1).

Reflexivity is especially vital when doing research in and about (trans)national contexts. Reflexivity is a form of "postcolonial theorizing" to approach the study of "cultural identities from the lenses of borderlands, hybridity, and diasporas" (Chen & Lin, 2016, Postcolonial Theory section, para. 1), which is why CIP connects (trans)national hybrid reflexivity with intersectionality. Following Jones and Calafell's (2012) work, it is crucial for (trans)national hybrids to engage in intersectional reflexivity to acknowledge how researchers' power and privilege can affect how they write about their own and other people's experiences. (Trans)national hybrid researchers could face unique challenges when engaging in reflexivity because they have to negotiate citizenship, nationality, and (un)documentation simultaneously as an intersectional performance of identities.

Ghabra and Calafell (2018) also remind me that it is important to recognize the relationship between power and reflexivity when communicating with Others, such as my role as a (trans)national Tsinoy researcher. Even though I was born and raised in the Philippines, living in the United States during my adult life has influenced my worldview and engagement with people. As Nakayama and Krizek (1995) note, "Reflexivity encourages an examination of the institutions and the politics that produce 'knowledge'" (p. 304); therefore, reflexivity should involve questioning one's theoretical and methodological approaches that are grounded primarily in U.S. and other Western epistemological perspectives. In fact, Miike (2003) raises the same concern:

> If critical intercultural communication scholars, most of whom are trained in highly privileged scholarly environments at European or U.S. universities, confine themselves to what might be termed Eurocentric approaches to anti-Eurocentrism by failing to examine their ideal version of humanity and to treat other Eurocentric intellectual traditions as resources of knowledge for theory-building, they will end up imposing pale imitations of Euro-American critical scholarship on other parts of the world and they will further perpetuate Eurocentric elitism. (p. 267)

Miike's point is valid, which is why I engage in (trans)national hybrid reflexivity by marking power differentials between researchers and participants. (Trans)national hybrid reflexivity is also about owning my Tsinoyness but also clearly acknowledging how my U.S. educational background could shape my perception and interpretation of Tsina/oy experiences.

Unpacking (Trans)national Tsina/oys

November 30, 2010. While getting ready for bed, my aunt checks in with me to see if I need anything else to make my stay comfortable. Before I get to answer her, my aunt walks directly to the side of the room and turns on the air conditioner. Knowing the humidity and heat in Manila can be unbearable even in

November, my aunt insists on leaving the air conditioner on throughout the night. The room has cooled down considerably about an hour later, so I turn the air conditioner off and hop on the bed to go to sleep. My jet-lagged body, however, keeps me up thinking about the anticipation of reuniting with family and friends. I also wonder about how my interpersonal interactions with them could bring back many childhood memories that would help me rediscover who I am.

Examining my Tsinoy identity is one aspect of why I am writing this book; it is also my intent to hear from other Tsina/oys to understand how Tsina/oyness functions as (trans)national hybridity in physical and online settings. I hope to accomplish my goals for this book with the subsequent chapters in mind. Chapter Two, "Documenting Tsina/oy Voices: Identities and Representation in (Trans)national Spaces," lays the foundation of my multimethodological ethnographic approach of using critical ethnographic interview, autoethnography, and cyberethnography to analyze Tsina/oy experiences culturally and socially. Chapter Three, "Performing Tsina/oyness: (E)merging Chinese and Filipina/o Identities," focuses on my critical ethnographic interviews of Tsina/oys in the Philippines. Emphasizing the intersectionality of nationality, ethnicity, and class, I investigate how Tsina/oys embody their Chinese and Filipina/o identities in different cultural contexts. In Chapter Four, "Becoming Tsinoy American: (Trans)national Identity and Citizenship," I share my autoethnographic journey of participating in the Oath of Allegiance ceremony to become a U.S. citizen while dealing with the tension of simultaneously gaining and losing a national identity. Chapter Five, "Virtually Tsina/oy: Performing Hybridity Online," features my cyberethnography of Tsinoy.com to examine its online members' communication of (trans)national Tsina/oy identity.[ii] I conclude the book with Chapter Six, "Generational Tsina/oys: (Auto)ethnographic Reflections and Future Directions." Drawing from my ethnographic interviews and autoethnographic reflections, I discuss the complexity of Tsina/oy identity across generations and its future as (trans)national hybridity in and beyond the Philippines. Collectively, these chapters exemplify the promise of a multimethodological approach to ethnography to narrate and represent diverse Tsina/oy experiences in (trans)national spaces.

Notes

i "Tsinoy" and "Filipino" are considered gender neutral in Tagalog language. Even though there is a movement in the United States to use "Filipinx" to represent gender fluid identities, it is not a localized term in the Philippines. To avoid imposing a U.S. American term while attempting to be gender inclusive, I use "Tsina/oy" and "Filipina/o" instead while recognizing their own limitations. Additionally, I did not alter any author's and participant's usage of "Tsinoy" and "Filipino."

ii Tsinoy.com was no longer available as of June 20, 2011.

References

Alexander, B. K. (2004). Passing, cultural performance, and individual agency: Performative reflections on black masculine identity. *Cultural Studies ↔ Critical Methodologies*, 4(3), 377–404. https://doi.org/10.1177/1532708603259680

Alexander, B. K. (2006). *Performing black masculinity: Race, culture, and queer identity*. AltaMira Press.

Alexander, B. K. (2017). "Black man/white tower": A performative film autocritography. In G. R. Musolf (Ed.), *Oppression and resistance: Structure, agency, transformation* (pp. 51–68). Emerald Publishing. https://doi.org/10.1108/S0163-239620170000048006

Alexander, B. K., Anderson, G. L., & Gallegos, B. P. (2005). Introduction: Performance in education. In B. K. Alexander, G. L. Anderson, & B. P. Gallegos (Eds.), *Performance theories in education: Power, pedagogy, and the politics of identity* (pp. 1–11). Lawrence Erlbaum Associates.

Alexander, B. K., Arasaratnam, L. A., Avant-Mier, R., Durham, A., Flores, L., Leeds-Hurwitz, W., Mendoza, S. L., Oetzel, J., Osland, J., Tsuda, Y., Yin, J., & Halualani, R. (2014). Defining and communicating what "intercultural" and "intercultural communication" means to us. *Journal of International & Intercultural Communication*, 7(1), 14–37. https://doi.org/10.1080/17513057.2014.869524

Anderson, B. (1998). Nationalism, identity, and the world-in-motion: On the logics of seriality. In P. Cheah & B. Robbins (Eds.), *Cosmopolitics: Thinking and feeling beyond the nation* (pp. 117–133). University of Minnesota Press.

Anthias, F. (1998). Evaluating 'diaspora': Beyond ethnicity? *Sociology*, 32(3), 557–580. https://doi.org/10.1177/0038038598032003009

Anthias, F. (2001). New hybridities, old concepts: The limits of "culture." *Ethnic and Racial Studies*, 24(4), 619–641. https://doi.org/10.1080/01419870120049815

Anzaldúa, G. (1999). *Borderlands/La frontera: The new mestiza* (2nd ed.). Aunt Lute Books.

Aparicio, F. R. (2004). U.S. Latino expressive cultures. In D. G. Gutiérrez (Ed.), *The Columbia history of Latinos in the United States since 1960* (pp. 355–390). Columbia University Press.

Appadurai, A. (1990). Disjuncture and difference in the global cultural economy. In P. Williams & L. Chrisman (Eds.), *Colonial discourse and post-colonial theory* (pp. 324–339). Columbia University Press.

Appadurai, A. (1996). *Modernity at large: Cultural dimensions of globalization*. University of Minnesota Press.

Bakhtin, M. M. (1981). *The dialogic imagination: Four essays* (C. Emerson & M. Holquist, Trans.). University of Texas Press.

Bardhan, N. (2011). Slumdog millionaire meets "India Shining": (Trans)national narrations of identity in South Asian diaspora. *Journal of International & Intercultural Communication*, 4(1), 42–61. https://doi.org/10.1080/17513057.2010.533785

Basch, L., Glick Schiller, N., & Szanton Blanc, C. (1995). *Nations unbound: Transnational projects, postcolonial predicaments, and deterritorialized nation-states*. Gordon and Breach Publishers.

Bautista, M. L. S. (2004). Tagalog-English code switching as a mode of discourse. *Asia Pacific Education Review*, 5(2), 226–233. https://doi.org/10.1007/BF03024960

Besserer, F. (2018). Transnational studies twenty years later: A story of encounters and disencounters. *Etnográfica*, 22(1), 109–130. https://doi.org/10.4000/etnografica.5172

Bhabha, H. (1994). *The location of culture*. Routledge. https://doi.org/10.4324/9780203820551

Brah, A. (1996). *Cartographies of the diaspora*. Routledge. https://doi.org/10.4324/9780203974919

Calafell, B. M. (2004). Disrupting the dichotomy: 'Yo soy Chicana/o?' in the new Latina/o south. *Communication Review*, 7(2), 175–204. https://doi.org/10.1080/10714420490448705

Calafell, B. M. (2005). Pro(re-)claiming loss: A performance pilgrimage in search of Malintzin Tenépal. *Text and Performance Quarterly*, 25(1), 43–56. https://doi.org/10.1080/10462930500052327

Calafell, B. M. (2007). *Latina/o communication studies: Theorizing performance*. Peter Lang.

Calafell, B. M. (2014). Performance: Keeping rhetoric honest. *Text and Performance Quarterly*, 34(1), 115–117. https://doi.org/10.1080/10462937.2013.846476

Calafell, B. M., Eguchi, S., & Abdi, S. (2020). Introduction: De-whitening intersectionality in intercultural communication. In S. Eguchi, B. M. Calafell, & S. Abdi (Eds.), *De-whitening intersectionality: Race, intercultural Communication, and politics* (pp. xvii–xxvii). Lexington Books.

Cariño, T. C. (1988). The Chinese in the Philippines: A survey of the literature. *Journal of the South Sea Society*, 43, 43–54.

Cariño, T. C. (2001). The Philippines. In E. T. Gomez & H.-H. M. Hsiao (Eds.), *Chinese business in Southeast Asia: Contesting cultural explanations, researching entrepreneurship* (pp. 101–123). Curzon.

Chen, Y.-W., & Lin, H. (2016). Cultural identities. In J. F. Nussbaum (Ed.), *Oxford research encyclopedia of communication*. Oxford University Press. https://doi.org/10.1093/acrefore/9780190228613.013.20

Cheng, H.-I. (2008). *Culturing interface: Identity, communication, and Chinese transnationalism*. Peter Lang.

Chrifi Alaoui, F. Z., & Calafell, B. M. (2016). A story of mentoring: From praxis to theory. In K. E. Tassie & S. M. Brown Givens (Eds.), *Critical examinations of women of color navigating mentoring relationships* (pp. 61–81). Lexington Books.

Chu, R. T. (2010). *Chinese and Chinese mestizos of Manila: Family, identity, and culture, 1860s-1930s*. Brill. https://doi.org/10.1163/ej.9789004173392.i-452

Chua, A. (2003). *World on fire: How exporting free market democracy breeds ethnic hatred and global instability*. First Anchor Books.

Clifford, J. (1994). Diasporas. *Cultural Anthropology*, 9(3), 302–338. https://doi.org/10.1525/can.1994.9.3.02a00040

Collier, M. J., Hegde, R. S., Lee, W. S., Nakayama, T. K., & Yep, G. A. (2001). Dialogue on the edges: Ferment in communication and culture. In M. J. Collier (Ed.), *Transforming communication about culture: Critical new directions* (pp. 219–280). SAGE. http://dx.doi.org/10.4135/9781452233208

Collins, P. H. (1990). *Black feminist thought: Knowledge, consciousness and the politics of empowerment*. Hyman.

Conquergood, D. (1991). Rethinking ethnography: Towards a critical cultural politics. *Communication Monographs, 58*(2), 179–194. https://doi.org/10.1080/03637759109376222

Córdoba, M. S. T. (2005). Sketches of identities from the Mexico-US border (or the other way around). *Comparative American Studies: An International Journal, 3*(4), 495–513. https://doi.org/10.1177/1477570005058963

Crenshaw, K. W. (1989). Demarginalizing the intersection of race and sex: A black feminist critique of antidiscrimination doctrine, feminist theory and antiracist politic. *University of Chicago Legal Forum, 1989*(1), 139–167.

Crenshaw, K. W. (1991). Mapping the margins: Intersectionality, identity politics, and violence against women of color. *Stanford Law Review, 43*(6), 1241–1299. https://doi.org/10.2307/1229039

de Certeau, M. (1984). *The practice of everyday life* (S. Rendall, Trans.). University of California Press.

Doeppers, D. F. (1986). Destination, selection and turnover among Chinese migrants to Philippine cities in the nineteenth century. *Journal of Historical Geography, 12*(4), 381–401. https://doi.org/10.1016/S0305-7488(86)80176-1

Drzewiecka, J. A. (2002). Reinventing and contesting identities in constitutive discourses: Between diaspora and its others. *Communication Quarterly, 50*(1), 1–23. https://doi.org/10.1080/01463370209385643

Eguchi, S. (2011). Cross-national identity transformation: Becoming a gay "Asian-American" man. *Sexuality & Culture, 15*(1), 19–40. https://doi.org/10.1007/s12119-010-9080-z

Eguchi, S. (2014). Ongoing cross-national identity transformation: Living on the queer Japan-U.S. transnational borderland. *Sexuality and Culture, 18*(4), 977–993. https://doi.org/10.1007/s12119-014-9234-5

Featherstone, M. (1995). *Undoing culture: Globalization, postmodernity, and identity*. SAGE. http://dx.doi.org/10.4135/9781446250457

Gajjala, R. (2004). *Cyber selves: Feminist ethnographies of South Asian women*. AltaMira Press.

García Canclini, N. (1995). *Hybrid cultures: Strategies for entering and leaving modernity* (C. L. Chiappari & S. L. Lopez, Trans.). University of Minnesota Press.

Ghabra, H., & Calafell, B. M. (2018). From failure and allyship to feminist solidarities: Negotiating our privileges and oppressions across borders. *Text and Performance Quarterly, 38*(1–2), 38–54. https://doi.org/10.1080/10462937.2018.1457173

Gilroy, P. (1993). *The black Atlantic: Modernity and double consciousness*. Harvard University Press.

Gómez-Peña, G. (1996). *The new world border: Prophesies, poems and loqueras for the end of the century*. City Lights.

Gonzales, W. D. W. (2016). Trilingual code-switching using quantitative lenses: An exploratory study on Hokaglish. *Philippine Journal of Linguistics, 47*, 109–131.

Gonzales, W. D. W. (2017). Language contact in the Philippines: The history and ecology from a Chinese Filipino perspective. *Language Ecology*, 1(2), 185–212. https://doi.org/10.1075/le.1.2.04gon

Gonzalez, A. (2004). The social dimensions of Philippine English. *World Englishes*, 23(1), 7–16. https://doi.org/10.1111/j.1467-971X.2004.00331.x

Gordon, N. S. (2016). Reggae 3.0: Social media and the consumption of Jamaican popular culture. In K. Sorrells & S. Sekimoto (Eds.), *Globalizing intercultural communication: A reader* (pp. 228–238). SAGE.

Greiner, C., & Sakdapolrak, P. (2013). Translocality: Concepts, applications and emerging research perspectives. *Geography Compass*, 7(5), 373–384. https://doi.org/10.1111/gec3.12048

Guéguen, C. (2010). Moving from Binondo to the "Chinese villages" of the suburbs: A geographical study of the Chinese in Metro-Manila. *Journal of Chinese Overseas*, 6(1), 119–137. https://doi.org/10.1163/179325410X491491

Hall, B. J. (1992). Theories of culture and communication. *Communication Theory*, 2(1), 50–70. https://doi.org/10.1111/j.1468-2885.1992.tb00028.x

Hall, S. (1996). New ethnicities. In D. Morley & K. Chen (Eds.), *Stuart Hall: Critical dialogues in cultural studies* (pp. 441–449). Routledge.

Halualani, R. T. (1998). Seeing through the screen: The struggle of culture. In J. N. Martin, T. K. Nakayama, & L. A. Flores (Eds.), *Readings in cultural contexts* (pp. 264–275). Mayfield Publishing.

Halualani, R. T. (2000). Rethinking "ethnicity" as structural-cultural project(s): Notes on the interface between cultural studies and intercultural communication. *International Journal of Intercultural Relations*, 24(5), 579–602. https://doi.org/10.1016/S0147-1767(00)00018-3

Halualani, R. T. (2008). "Where exactly is the Pacific?": Global migrations, diasporic movements, and intercultural communication. *Journal of International and Intercultural Communication*, 1(1), 3–22. https://doi.org/10.1080/17513050701739509

Halualani, R. T., Mendoza, S. L., & Drzewiecka, J. A. (2009). "Critical" junctures in intercultural communication studies: A review. *The Review of Communication*, 9(1), 17–35. https://doi.org/10.1080/15358590802169504

Halualani, R. T., & Nakayama, T. K. (2010). Critical intercultural communication studies at a crossroads. In T. K. Nakayama & R. T. Halualani (Eds.), *The handbook of critical intercultural communication* (pp. 1–16). Wiley-Blackwell. https://doi.org/10.1002/9781444390681

Hao, R. N. (2012). Cultural reentry: A critical review of intercultural communication research. In N. Bardhan & M. O. Orbe (Eds.), *Identity research and communication* (pp. 71–85). Lexington Books.

Hao, R. N. (2013). Virtually Tsina/oy: Performing and negotiating diasporic hybridity online. *Qualitative Communication Research*, 2(2), 159–181. https://doi.org/10.1525/qcr.2013.2.2.159

Hao, R. N. (2020). Critical intercultural performance framework: Transnational hybridity as performance of reentries. *Journal of Intercultural Communication Research*, 49(5), 425–432. https://doi.org/10.1080/17475759.2020.1798804

Hau, C. S. (2005). Conditions of visibility: Resignifying the "Chinese"/"Filipino" in *Mano Po* and *Crying Ladies*. *Philippine Studies*, 53(4), 491–531.

Hegde, R. (2002). Translated enactments: The relational configurations of the Asian Indian immigrant experience. In J. N. Martin, T. K. Nakayama, & L. A. Flores (Eds.), *Readings in intercultural communication: Experiences and contexts* (2nd ed., pp. 259–266). McGraw-Hill.

hooks, b. (1981). *Ain't I a woman*. South End Press.

hooks, b. (1990). *Yearning: Race, gender, and cultural politics*. South End Press.

Johnson, A. L., & LeMaster, B. (Eds.). (2020). *Gender futurity, Intersectional autoethnography: Embodied theorizing from the margins*. Routledge.

Jones Jr., R. G., & Calafell, B. M. (2012). Contesting neoliberalism through critical pedagogy, intersectional reflexivity, and personal narrative: Queer tales of academia. *Journal of Homosexuality, 59*(7), 957–981. https://doi.org/10.1080/00918369.2012.699835

Joseph, M. (1999). Introduction: New hybrid identities and performance. In M. Joseph & J. N. Fink (Eds.), *Performing hybridity* (pp. 1–24). University of Minnesota Press.

Klöter, H. (2011). *The language of the Sangleys: A Chinese vernacular in missionary sources of the seventeenth century*. Brill. https://doi.org/10.1163/9789004195929

Kraidy, M. M. (2002). Hybridity in cultural globalization. *Communication Theory, 12*(3), 316–339. https://doi.org/10.1111/j.1468-2885.2002.tb00272.x

Kraidy, M. M. (2005). *Hybridity, or the cultural logic of globalization*. Temple University Press.

Leeds-Hurwitz, W. (1990). Notes on the history of intercultural communication: The Foreign Service Institute and the mandate for intercultural training. *Quarterly Journal of Speech, 76*(3), 262–281. https://doi.org/10.1080/00335639009383919

Levitt, P., & Jaworsky, B. N. (2007). Transnational migration studies: Past developments and future trends. *Annual Review of Sociology, 33*, 129–156. https://doi.org/10.1146/annurev.soc.33.040406.131816

Madison, D. S., & Hamera, J. (2006). Performance studies at the intersections. In D. S. Madison & J. Hamera (Eds.), *The SAGE handbook of performance studies* (pp. xi–xxv). SAGE.

Martin, J. N., & Nakayama, T. K. (1999). Thinking about culture dialectically. *Communication Theory, 9*(1), 1–25. https://doi.org/10.1111/j.1468-2885.1999.tb00160.x

McIntosh, D. M., & Hobson, K. (2013). Reflexive engagement: A white (queer) women's performance of failures and alliance possibilities. *Liminalities: A Journal of Performance Studies, 9*(4), 1–23. http://liminalities.net/9-4/reflexive.pdf

Miike, Y. (2003). Beyond Eurocentrism in the intercultural field: Searching for an Asiacentric paradigm. In W. J. Starosta & G. M. Chen (Eds.), *Ferment in the intercultural field: Axiology/value/praxis* (pp. 243–276). SAGE.

Molina Guzmán, I., & Valdivia, A. N. (2004) Brain, brow or bootie: Iconic Latinas in contemporary popular culture. *Communication Review, 7*(2), 205–221. https://doi.org/10.1080/10714420490448723

Moon, D. G. (1996). Concepts of 'culture': Implications for intercultural communication research. *Communication Quarterly, 44*(1), 70–84. https://doi.org/10.1080/01463379609370001

Moreman, S. T. (2008). Hybrid performativity, south and north of the border: Entre La Teoría Y La Materialidad De Hibridación. In A. N. Valdivia (Ed.), *Latina/o communication studies today* (pp. 91–111). Peter Lang.

Naficy, H. (1993). *The making of exile cultures: Iranian television in Los Angeles*. University of Minnesota Press.

Nakayama, T. K., & Krizek, R. L. (1995). Whiteness: A strategic rhetoric. *Quarterly Journal of Speech, 81*(3), 291–309. https://doi.org/10.1080/00335639509384117

Nurse, K. (1999). Globalization and Trinidad carnival: Diaspora, hybridity and identity in global culture. *Cultural Studies, 13*(4), 661–690. https://doi.org/10.1080/095023899335095

Ono, K. A. (1998). Problematizing "nation" in intercultural communication research. In D. Tanno & A. Gonzalez (Eds.), *Communication and identity across cultures* (pp. 34–55). SAGE.

Pascual, M. R. (2004). Traversing disparate cultures in a transnational world. In A. González, M. Houston, & V. Chen (Eds.), *Our voices: Essays on culture, ethnicity, and communication* (4th ed., pp. 288–297). Roxbury Publishing.

Rivera, T. C., & Koike, K. (1995). *The Chinese-Filipino business families under the Ramos government*. Institute for Developing Economies.

Rosaldo, R. (1989). *Cultural and truth: The remaking of social analysis*. Beacon Press.

Safran, W. (1991). Diasporas in modern societies: Myths of homeland and return. *Diaspora: A Journal of Transnational Studies, 1*(1), 83–99. https://doi.org/10.1353/dsp.1991.0004

See, T. A. (1997a). *Chinese in the Philippines: Problems & perspectives* (Vol. 1). Kaisa Para Sa Kaunlaran.

See, T. A. (1997b). *Chinese in the Philippines: Problems & perspectives* (Vol. 2). Kaisa Para Sa Kaunlaran.

See, T. A. (2004). *Chinese in the Philippines: Problems & perspectives* (Vol. 3). Kaisa Para Sa Kaunlaran.

See, T. A. (2016). The ethnic Chinese in Korea and in the Philippines: An exploratory study. *Translocal Chinese: East Asian Perspectives, 10*(1), 93–120. https://doi.org/10.1163/24522015-01001005

Shi, Y. (2005). Identity construction of the Chinese diaspora, ethnic media use, community formation, and the possibility of social activism. *Continuum: Journal of Media & Cultural Studies, 19*(1), 55–72. https://doi.org/10.1080/1030431052000336298

Shome, R. (1996). Postcolonial interventions in the rhetorical canon: An "other" view. *Communication Theory, 6*(1), 40–59. https://doi.org/10.1111/j.1468-2885.1996.tb00119.x

Shugart, H. A. (2007). Crossing over: Hybridity and hegemony in the popular media. *Communication and Critical/Cultural Studies, 4*(2), 115–141. https://doi.org/10.1080/14791420701296505

Sy, J. (2015). Scholarships and education projects in the Chinese Filipino community: An overview. *Chinese Studies Program Lecture Series, 2*, 1–14.

Tan, A. S. (1988). The changing identity of the Philippine Chinese, 1946-1984. In J. Cushman & G. Wang (Eds.), *Changing identities of the Southeast Asian Chinese since World War II* (pp. 177–203). Hong Kong University Press.

Tan, S. V. (1972). *The Chinese in the Philippines, 1898–1935: A study of their national awakening*. Garcia Publishing Co.

Thompson, R. M. (2003). Filipino English and Taglish: Language switching from multiple perspectives. John Benjamins. https://doi.org/10.1075/veaw.g31

Tölölyan, K. (1996). Rethinking diaspora(s): Stateless power in the transnational moment. *Diaspora: A Journal of Transnational Studies, 5*(1), 3–36. https://doi.org/10.1353/dsp.1996.0000

Turner, V. W. (1969). *The ritual process: Structure and anti-structure.* AldineTransaction.

Tyrrell, I. (2001). New comparisons, international worlds: Transnational and comparative perspectives. *Australian Feminist Studies, 16*(36): 355–361. https://doi.org/10.1080/08164640120097570

Uytanlet, J. L. (2016). *The hybrid Tsinoys: Challenges of hybridity and homogeneity as socio-cultural constructs among the Chinese in the Philippines.* Pickwick Publications.

Vertovec, S. (1997). Three meanings of "diaspora," exemplified by South Asian religions. *Diaspora: A Journal of Transnational Studies, 6*(3), 277–299. https://doi.org/10.1353/dsp.1997.0010

Warren, J. T. (2008). Performing difference: Repetition in context. *Journal of International and Intercultural Communication, 1*(4), 290–308. https://doi.org/10.1080/17513050802344654

Warren, J. T., & Fassett, D. (2002). (Re)constituting ethnographic identities. *Qualitative Inquiry, 8*(5), 575–590. https://doi.org/10.1177/107780002237005

Wickberg, E. (1965). *The Chinese in Philippine Life, 1850–1898.* Yale University Press.

Yap, J. P. (2018). The troubled dual construction of ethnicity of recent Chinese migrants and third generation Chinese-Filipinos in Binondo, Manila. *Mabini Review, 7,* 166–198.

Yep, G. A. (2002). My three cultures: Navigating the multicultural identity landscape. In J. Martin, T. Nakayama, & L. Flores (Eds.), *Readings in intercultural communication: Experiences and contexts* (2nd ed., pp. 60–66). McGraw-Hill.

Yep, G. A. (2016). Toward thick(er) intersectionalities: Theorizing, researching, and activating the complexities of communication and identities. In K. Sorrells & S. Sekimoto (Eds.), *Globalizing intercultural communication: A reader* (pp. 86–94). SAGE.

Young, S. L. (2009). Half and half: An (auto)ethnography of hybrid identities in a Korean American mother-daughter relationship. *Journal of International and Intercultural Communication, 2*(2), 139–167. https://doi.org/10.1080/17513050902759512

Yu, J. V. B. (2000). *Inculturation of Filipino-Chinese culture mentality.* Editrice Pontificia Universita Gregoriana.

DOCUMENTING TSINA/OY VOICES: IDENTITIES AND REPRESENTATION IN (TRANS)NATIONAL SPACES

December 1, 2010. After a sleepless night, I crawl out of bed to start my second day in Manila. I enter the living room where my 95-year-old grandmother awaits my presence. While watching TV in her armchair, I greet my grandmother, who instructs me to go to the kitchen immediately to eat breakfast. I notice that my aunt left some pastries on the kitchen table. I pick up the familiar *ma sung*-topped bun (dry shredded pork bun) and pair it with a cup of instant coffee. Eating my breakfast, I can't help but look around the kitchen space that remains largely unchanged from when I used to frequent it as a child. From the fluorescent ceiling light to the breakfast nook area, the kitchen serves as a reminder of a space where my grandmother prepared home cooked meals for the whole family gathering to celebrate holidays and other important occasions.

As I take my seat on the couch with a full stomach, my grandmother asks if I had a good night's sleep. Without hesitation, I tell her that I did, even though my body has not quite adjusted to a 16-hour time difference. Waking up past 9 a.m., it is considered a late start for my grandmother who always gets up before the sun rises. With the TV on, my grandmother is preoccupied with today's current events as she reads the local Chinese newspaper. Noticing that I am not saying much, she puts down the newspaper on her lap and strikes a conversation with me. Recalling my favorite Tsina/oy pastry, she asks whether I want to get an *ube hopia* (flaky pastry made with purple yam), which can be purchased within a few blocks from my grandmother's apartment in the heart of Manila's Chinatown. Insisting that I can get the *hopia* later, my grandmother continues the conversation by asking about what I plan to do today. I share with my grandmother that I need to discuss with my aunt, who serves as my informant, about my book project. My grandmother is naturally curious about my book. Without getting into too much detail and keeping the topic as accessible as possible, I tell her that the book is about the Chinese in the Philippines. Even with my explanation of what the book is about, my grandmother shows excitement knowing that I am doing an important scholarly work.

A few hours later, my aunt finally comes home from work. She greets me and my grandmother upon entering the living room. She sits down on the couch next to me and is eager to talk about my research project. Having known about my plan to write a book about Tsina/oys, she reminds my grandmother about my research and the need to schedule interviews to document experiences of other Tsina/oys. I also explain to them the formal process of providing a consent form to ask participants' permission to be interviewed. Intrigued with the questions I will ask my participants, I speak in a combination of Taglish and Hokkien with my aunt and grandmother that the interview questions will focus on participants' understanding of "Tsina/oy" identity and how they negotiate their Chinese and Filipina/o identities in different cultural and social contexts.

My personal quest to learn more about what it means to be Tsina/oy started in 2007 while attending graduate school in Carbondale, Illinois, a small rural Midwestern college town in the United States. It was the first time I lived outside of the Los Angeles suburbs where I grew up experiencing both Chinese and Filipina/o cultures. Because I could no longer find a homeplace (hooks, 1994) of cultural familiarity in Carbondale, I especially longed for a Tsina/oy community to (re)discover my Tsinoyness. Not knowing what to expect, I turned to the Web to search "Tsinoy" to see what kind of results I would find. To my surprise, I found Tsinoy.com and subsequently engaged in a cyberethnography of the online community where Tsina/oys around the world could (re)connect with other Tsina/oy participants.

Finding a Tsina/oy community online inspired me to examine Tsina/oy identity further by conducting interviews in the Philippines. By examining various Tsina/oy voices in the Philippines and online, as well as reflecting from my own lived experiences, I provide in this chapter an overview of critical ethnographic interview, autoethnography, and cyberethnography as methodological tools to document and analyze what it means to be Tsina/oy culturally and socially. Similar to Alexander's (1999) work, I engage in a multimethodological approach that exemplifies "variations of the primary method of ethnography" (p. 308) to offer unique and multiple perspectives of examining Tsina/oy identity. Combining these ethnographic methods "yields a wealth of articulated knowledge" (p. 308), specifically by allowing me and other Tsina/oy "participants to articulate [our] stories in ways that are reflective of [our] lived experience" (p. 308) in both (trans)national physical and online spaces.

Critical Ethnographic Interview: Performing Tsina/oy Lives

December 1, 2010. After satisfying my aunt and grandmother's query about the interview process, I tell them politely that I will be heading back into the guest bedroom. I take out a folder from my backpack that contains paper-clipped copies of consent forms for my interviews. I sit on the bed, thinking about the first time I will be conducting interviews in the Philippines. Even though I find comfort knowing that I will be interviewing Tsina/oys, I feel nervous about meeting them and their initial perceptions of me. Would they find it interesting that I am conducting research on Tsina/oy identity? Would they warm up to me knowing that I am Tsinoy? Would it matter to them that I came from the United States? As I ponder through these thoughts, I am hopeful that the rewards of hearing Tsina/oy voices will outweigh my challenges as a critical ethnographic interviewer.

Ethnography is a method that aids "researchers to understand how others view their experience" (Stage & Mattson, 2003, p. 99) and document it as a "written representation of culture" (VanMaanen, 1988, p. 1). Ethnography, as Hammersley (1990) explains, involves a researcher who enters a site and observes or participates in activities to learn about a culture. As a process, ethnographers go through the stages of obtaining access, gathering data, and conducting the analysis (Hammersley & Atkinson, 1995). Ethnographic data collection includes interviews, descriptions, and excerpts of documents (Hammersley, 1990). Hammersley (1990) adds that ethnography usually has the following features: (a) people's behaviors are studied in everyday contexts, (b) data consist of observation or informal conversations, (c) data collection is typically unstructured and does not involve detailed planning, (d) the focus of research is usually one group or setting, and (e) data analysis takes the form of interpreting the meanings and functions of verbal and nonverbal behaviors.

Unlike traditional approaches to ethnography, critical ethnography makes an explicit commitment to challenge power relations and inequalities that exist in different contexts (Thomas, 1993). With critique at its core, critical ethnography is "a perspective that provides fundamental images, metaphors, and understandings about our social world" (Thomas, 2003, p. 46). Influenced by anthropology and sociology (Thomas, 1993), ethnographers began exploring ways to infuse critical acts in their research in the 1960s and 1970s (Noblit et al., 2004), which were primarily drawn from Marxist and neo-Marxist theoretical perspectives (Carspecken, 1996). Ongoing social movements to create awareness and fight against gender, racial, and postcolonial injustice expanded critical ethnography's epistemological trajectories (Levinson & Holland, 1996; Villenas & Foley, 2002). Consequently, critical theory emerged and situated itself informing critical ethnography as a method (Kinchloe & McLaren, 2000). Hence, critical ethnography "becomes the 'doing'—or, better, the performance—of critical theory" (Madison, 2005, p. 13). Integrating critical theory with political and pedagogical approaches to ethnography (Simon & Dippo, 1986), critical ethnography examines and critiques ideologies and societies rooted in historical, political, and institutional formations (Marcus & Fischer, 1986).

At the heart of critical ethnography is engaging in in-depth interviewing of participants, which aims "to describe and understand the unique experiences of others" (Stage & Mattson, 2003, p. 97), especially those who are "restrained and out of reach" (Madison, 2005, p. 5). Ethnographic interviews can occur in three ways: oral history, personal narrative, and topic interview. According to Madison (2005), oral history recounts "a social historical moment reflected the life or lives of individuals who remember them and/or experienced them" (p. 26). A personal narrative is based on a person's perspective to share the happening of an "event, experience, or point of view" (p. 26). Finally, a topical interview takes place when an individual provides a perspective on a "particular subject, such as a program, an issue, or a process" (p. 26). While each type of ethnographic interview is distinguished, it is possible for all of them to overlap simultaneously in an interview project.

Critical ethnographic interviews serve as dialogic exchanges between researcher and participants "to construct memory, meaning, and experience together" (Madison, 2005, p. 25). Methodologically, qualitative researchers must be able to state the study's purpose, ask a research question, describe the population for research, establish a time period for study, gather and evaluate data, and present findings (Glesne, 1999). Altogether in December 2010 and June 2011, I engaged in critical ethnographic interviews with 32 Tsina/oys in Manila and surrounding cities to analyze their communication of (trans)national and intersectional Chinese and Filipina/o identities as hybrid performances in different facets of their everyday life. My aunt served as my informant, who facilitated meetings with community members and participants (Mattson & Stage, 2003). Of the 32 participants (all identified with a pseudonym), 19 were women and 13 were men between 21 and 72 years of age. Twenty-four participants considered themselves as working professionals, and eight of them were recent college graduates. Depending on the preference of participants, interviews were held in residences, offices, coffee shops, and restaurants. Each interview lasted approximately one hour.

December 1, 2010. It is approaching dinner time, and my aunt shares with me enthusiastically that she managed to secure two interviews for me later tonight. I will be interviewing two residents from our same apartment building after dinner. After finishing our meal, my aunt reminds me to bring my audio recorder. Taking the elevator, my aunt and I arrive at the well-lit rooftop terrace where Denisa sits at a table patiently. No one else is around the terrace wherever I turn. My aunt greets Denisa warmly, and I follow up by shaking her hand. A few minutes later, Vivian arrives and checks in with me and my aunt if the interview has already started. My aunt shakes her head from left to right, signaling "no" to Vivian. Even though I am prepared to do a joint interview with Denisa and Vivian, they are perfectly fine to be interviewed separately. In this case, Denisa proceeds to be interviewed first; Vivian chats with my aunt at the other side of the table while waiting for her turn.

Following Spradley's (1979) recommendation, I introduced myself as a Tsinoy researcher before starting the interview and stated the purpose of the project with my participants to understand what it means to be "Tsina/oy" and how it shapes their Chinese and Filipina/o identities through cultural, social, and linguistic practices. It is also essential for the ethnographer to explain to participants the interview process, topics that will be discussed, use of language, and mode of recording responses. To that end, I furnished my participants a copy of the consent form summarizing the process, specifying voluntary participation in the interview, using an audio recorder to document their experiences, emphasizing confidentiality by using pseudonyms, and providing contact information for additional questions and concerns about the project.

With proper protocol in place, the ethnographer employs different questions that are descriptive in nature focusing on events, people, space, time, events, or objects (Spradley, 1979). When conducting interviews, I asked my Tsina/oy participants questions addressing the following topics: demographic information (e.g., age, profession, birthplace, citizenship, family's cultural background), meaning of and identification with Chinese and Filipina/o identity, Tsina/oy cultural traditions and practices, spoken language(s), socialization and stereotype of Tsina/oys, and multiple tensions experienced while embodying Chinese and Filipina/o identities.

Moreover, I communicated clearly with my participants that I would be asking questions in English accompanied with translations in Tagalog and Hokkien whenever necessary, which means they could respond in any of the three languages during the interview. In practice, as Spradley (1979) notes, the ethnographer should encourage participants to speak in their own language. Speaking with participants in language(s) they are comfortable with is one of the ways for both interviewer and interviewee to engage in conversations organically (Rubin & Rubin, 1995). Ethnographic interviews should be treated like contextualized conversations where both interviewer and interviewee act as participants partaking in interviews that are reciprocal in nature (Stage & Mattson, 2003). Conquergood (1982) reminds us: "The power dynamic of the research situation changes when the ethnographer moves from the gaze to the distance and detached observer to the intimate involvement and engagement of 'coactivity' or co-performance" (pp. 12–13). In other words, a critical ethnographic interviewer is present in the moment with the participants to listen to and learn with them, even if the conversations get off topic (Mattson & Stage, 2003).

After conducting the interviews, the ethnographer transcribes and codes the interviews for analysis. The transcription process proved to be challenging, especially given the fact that my participants were multilingual. Many Tsina/oy participants spoke Tagalog, Hokkien, and English simultaneously. To ensure accuracy of transcription for Tagalog words, I consulted the Tagalog Dictionary website (https://www.tagalog-dictionary.com/). I also transcribed participants' Hokkien messages by referring primarily to Maryknoll Language Service Center's Taiwanese Dictionary (http://www.taiwanesedictionary.org). However, because Hokkien spoken in the Manila metropolitan area is a variant of the Taiwanese language, I also drew from MacGowan's *English and Chinese Dictionary of the Amoy Dialect* (1883) as another source.

Completing the transcription process means that I can finally read and interpret my participants' responses. Unlike survey research where researchers generate results based on "analytical categories," as an ethnographer, I "take the form of open-ended verbal descriptions in fieldnotes, of transcriptions of audio- or video-recordings, extracts of text from documents, etc." to formulate themes for analysis (Hammersley & Atkinson, 1995, p. 208). With careful reading of participants' responses, my ethnographic analysis involves identifying patterns or themes (Carspecken, 1996; Glesne, 1999) that represent a "cultural portrait" of "how the cultural group works and lives" (Cresswell, 2007, p. 72). As part of the ethnographic analysis process, Hammersley and Atkinson (1995) add the need to develop "a set of analytic categories that capture relevant aspects of these data, and the assignment of particular items of data to those categories" (pp. 208–209).

Beyond the transcription process and analysis, "representing Others is always going to be a complicated and contentious undertaking" (Madison, 2005, pp. 3–4). When writing, the way we communicate, perform, and use language is a reflexive act (Fassett & Warren, 2007). While reflection is an act of looking back to what was said when and to whom, reflexion is "an ongoing effort to call out, to illuminate, the (re)creation of our selves, our values, assumptions, and practices" (p. 50). In essence, reflexivity is the constant questioning of social locations and subjectivities that influence our worldviews and perspectives (Alexander, 2011; Conquergood, 1991; Goltz, 2011; Kincheloe & McLaren, 2000; McIntosh & Eguchi, 2020; Meyerhoff, 1981).

December 1, 2010. My first two interviews with Denisa and Vivian have concluded and made me cognizant of what it means to be reflexive. Both seemed to enjoy conversing with me about their experiences. They commended me for doing the interviews to learn more about Tsina/oy identity. Turning to me as a researcher, Denisa now seeks confirmation that I am a college professor. Before I get to say anything, my aunt responds proudly in Hokkien: "*I sī an Bí-kok kà chheh*" ["He teaches in the United States"]. However, Denisa misinterprets my aunt in Tagalog: "*Ah, Bikol ba?*" ["Oh, in Bikol (Philippines)?"]. My aunt interjects quickly in Hokkien: "*Bô la! Bí-kok! USA*" ["No! United States! USA"]. Denisa exclaims in Hokkien: "Wow! *Ya gaw*" ["Wow! Very good"]. I find the interaction between my aunt and Denisa amusing. I smile as I watch my aunt and Denisa's various cultural performances of what it means to be proud of a Tsinoy like me.

In the midst of the exchange between my aunt and Denisa, I can't help but think about how my professional background in the United States has established my privileged identity as a (trans)national Tsinoy. With that privilege, I am mindful to not boast about that part of my identity, although it is critical to acknowledge how my professional identity can impact others' perception of me. To question our social locations and subjectivities, Madison (2005) calls attention to the importance of researcher positionality as power, privilege, and biases. It is important to note that subjectivity and positionality are not the same; the former addresses the researcher's background, while the latter refers to the politics of speaking and writing about Others (Alcoff, 1991). As ethnographers who are representing other voices, Alcoff (1991) emphasizes that they must "interrogate the bearing of our location and context on what it is we are saying, and this should be an explicit part of every serious discursive practice we engage in" (p. 25). Regardless of intent, ethnographers have a responsibility to acknowledge who they are, their perspective, and the implications of their work on others.

Although ethnographers may write about cultural members in which they identify with, they must also consider how their experiences reflect those of the people sharing their narratives (Boylorn, 2011; Calafell, 2013). Due to our diverse and complex experiences, engaging in intersectional reflexivity "requires one to acknowledge one's intersecting identities, both marginalized and privileged, and then employ self-reflexivity, which moves one beyond self-reflection to the often uncomfortable level of self-implication" (Jones, 2010, p. 122). As a (trans)national Tsinoy, my experiences are unique from other Tsina/oys when moving across (trans)national spaces. Paying attention to the intersectionality of nationality, citizenship, and (un)documented bodies, my privileged body gives me a tremendous amount of power to move freely. Furthermore, centering the subjectivity of hybrid scholars, I acknowledge that reflexivity is to perform both privileged and marginalized identities that affect knowledge and experiences. With that in mind, reflexivity is "not just as an act that is private and personal, but public and plural; an outing of the self that implicates others" (Alexander, 2011, p. 105).

The Critical I: Examining the Cultural Self

December 2, 2010. As a (trans)national Tsinoy visiting the Philippines, my aunt suggests going to Bahay Tsinoy, a Chinese Filipina/o museum, this afternoon. I show enthusiasm by joining my aunt for a field trip. Bahay Tsinoy, which literally means "Chinese Filipino House," did not exist when I was a child in the Philippines. Feeling excited about the field trip, my aunt and I head out to Intramuros, an area of Manila filled with historic Spanish colonial architecture.

As we are pulling up to the museum's building, I am beyond ecstatic. This is the first time I am visiting a museum site that is dedicated to the history of Tsina/oys, legitimizing our presence in and contributions to the Philippines.

Standing inside Bahay Tsinoy is an incredible feeling. I am impressed with the museum's variety of collections—from historical documents to wax sculptures to cultural artifacts—representing Tsina/oy lives. Beyond the aesthetics of the museum, there is so much to see and learn. I walk gingerly to make sure I'm not overlooking anything. Suddenly, I am caught off guard standing in front of wax sculptures of native and Chinese individuals trading in the Philippines before Spanish colonialism, which shows the lengthy presence of the Chinese in the Philippines. As I continue my trip to the past, I learn about the (un)documentation of Tsina/oys that resulted in their historical struggles to be accepted in Philippine society. Bahay Tsinoy is not merely a space filled with artifacts as one would think of a museum in a literal sense, but it is "home" (hence, Tagalog for *bahay*) to remember Tsina/oys for their hybrid performances that have shaped them personally and culturally. Bahay Tsinoy also serves as a cultural site for me to remember what it means to be Tsinoy. Hence, I turn to autoethnography to specifically locate my body and share how my lived experiences connect to culture (Boylorn & Orbe, 2014, 2021; Chang, 2008; Ellis, 2004). Employing critical ethnographic interview and cyberethnography in my Tsina/oy research, autoethnography works well with other critical methods to offer a diverse representation of intersectional voices (Boylorn & Orbe, 2021).

Autoethnography is a method that "combines characteristics of autobiography and ethnography" (Ellis et al., 2011, p. 275). Like other "automethods," autoethnography blurs "the line between the ethnographic self and ethnographic other" (Pensoneau-Conway & Toyosaki, 2011, p. 385). As Alexander (2011) argues, autoethnography is "never just about me" but a constant fluid movement between self and culture (p. 100). At its core, autoethnography is "an approach to research and writing that seeks to describe and systematically analyze (graphy) personal experience (auto) in order to understand cultural experience (ethno)" (Ellis et al., 2011, p. 273) and critique the conditions of the culture in which self is located (Banks & Banks, 2000). Autoethnography also focuses on "defining of one's subjective ethnicity as mediated through language, history, and ethnographical analysis; in short...a kind of 'figural anthropology' of the self" (Lionnet, 1989, p. 99), which allows writers to document their own lived experiences within a specific cultural context (Alexander, 1999).

As a methodological approach that situates the researcher's body both as "research instrument" and site (Banks & Banks, 2000, p. 234), Holman Jones (2005) describes autoethnography as research and writing process by

> setting a scene, telling a story, weaving intricate connections among life and art, experience and theory, evocation and explanation…and then letting go, hoping for readers who will bring the same careful attention to your words in the context of their own lives. (p. 765)

In addition to its creative form, autoethnographers refer to fieldnotes, interviews, and/or other cultural artifacts to describe rich inter/personal experiences in the form of a narrative (Ellis, 2004). The detailed inter/personal accounts make it possible for participants and readers of autoethnography to observe and testify about a particular experience (Greenspan, 1998). With autoethnography, researchers "retrospectively and selectively write about epiphanies that stem from, or are made possible by, being part of a culture and/or by possessing a particular cultural identity" and analyze such experiences (Ellis et al., 2011, p. 276).

Historically, autoethnography as a method can be credited to Zora Neale Hurston for her "self-portrait" work in *Dust Tracks on a Road* (Lionnet, 1989, p. 98). By name, autoethnography can be traced back formally to the 1970s in which cultural members share a perspective of their culture (Hayano, 1979; Heider, 1975) that highlights personal observations, views, and voices (Goldschmidt, 1977). However, none of these early "autoethnographic" studies "explicitly foregrounded the inclusion and importance of personal experience in research" (Adams et al., 2017, p. 1). To counter traditional social science research that relies heavily on its objective stance, many qualitative and interpretive researchers in the 1980s advocated for autoethnography to emphasize the telling of personal narratives and how they can inform cultural ways of knowing (Adams et al., 2017; Ellis et al., 2011). More importantly, citing Ellis and Bochner (2000), many social scientists

> wanted to concentrate on ways of producing meaningful, accessible, and evocative research grounded in personal experience, research that would sensitize readers to issues of identity politics, to experiences shrouded in silence, and to forms of representation that deepen our capacity to empathize with people who are different from us. (Ellis et al., 2011, p. 274)

Knowing the limitations of traditional social science research, many scholars favored autoethnography because it is a form of research that recognizes different people have multitude ways of speaking and writing culturally (Ellis et al., 2011). Autoethnography, in this case, challenged what is considered valid research and created outlets to study topics that otherwise would not have been examined before.

Autoethnography emerged as a methodological choice for many communication scholars in the 1990s (and beyond) to utilize personal narrative that intersects with culture and reflexivity (e.g., Ellis, 1995, 2004; Ellis & Flaherty, 1992). Autoethnography has been linked with other names, such as autobiographical ethnography (Reed-Danahay, 1997), critical autobiography (Church, 1995), and confessional tales (Van Maanen, 1988), to name a few. The 1990s generated autoethnographers to take a critical approach that prompted many of them to write from feminist, indigenous, and native perspectives (Ellis & Bochner, 2000). Since then, critical scholars have utilized autoethnography to address decolonial (e.g., Chawla & Atay, 2018; Toyosaki, 2018), postcolonial (e.g., Dutta & Basu, 2013; Pathak, 2013), queer (e.g., Alexander, 2006; Calafell, 2013; Homan Jones & Adams, 2010; Spieldenner & Eguchi, 2020), and transnational (e.g., Eguchi, 2015; Hao, 2021) experiences.

Recognizing various approaches to autoethnography, I chose critical autoethnography to gain a performative understanding of my Tsinoy identity in (trans)national contexts. Referring to Conquergood (1991), critical autoethnography is a method that utilizes the performative body as a form of knowledge where movement, speech, feeling, and touch, among others, can provide insights to personal and cultural experiences of marginalized groups (Holman Jones, 2018). Because "the minority's voice is always personal" (Trinh, 1989, p. 28), critical autoethnography is especially vital as a methodological choice for those on the margins to critique social injustices and communicate commitments to change them (Adams, 2017). As such, autoethnography, especially from a critical perspective, can challenge dominant cultural narratives and stereotypes in ethnographic representations (Boylorn, 2014). Because of its commitments to the performative body and voice, I employ critical autoethnography in my work to serve as "a method that allows for both personal and cultural critique" (Boylorn & Orbe, 2021, p. 5) to investigate power relations in a cultural context.

Critical autoethnography also emphasizes the acknowledgment of intersectional identities and experiences (Holman Jones, 2018). Intersectionality is an important concept in autoethnography because it communicates how multiple identities—both privileged and disadvantaged—can be performed and negotiated simultaneously (e.g., Berry, 2016; Calafell, 2007, 2013; Griffin,

2012). Emphasizing intersectionality in critical autoethnography makes it possible for "'bleeding borders' or 'bleeding identities'" to travel across various places and spaces (Alexander, 2021, p. 32). Additionally, Calafell et al.'s (2020) work on de-whitening intersectionality is instrumental in a method like critical autoethnography because they reconceptualize intersectionality in ways that explicate, elucidate, and elaborate culture- and text-specific nuances of knowledge for women of color, queer/trans-people of color, and non-western people of color who have been marked as Others.

While writing autoethnographically, critical autoethnographers also acknowledge their privileges and marginalization simultaneously through the process of reflexivity (Boylorn & Orbe, 2021). Autoethnographers must "recognize the challenges that subjectivity brings and do what they can to understand and communicate how their assumptions, biases, and experiences affect the research" (Deitering, 2017, p. 15). Due to the constant movement between our locations and subjectivities, reflexivity is "always a vulnerable act. It is vulnerable because the process exposes that which is always being concealed in scholarly research and particularly in ethnographic research" (Alexander, 2011, p. 105). As a Tsinoy interacting with Tsina/oy participants, I "entered familiar spaces" with "my own voice as a cultural familiar" (p. 99). However, acknowledging my U.S. educational background and (trans)national identity is always a reflexive act. It is also not uncommon for autoethnographers to experience tensions and doubts (Douglas & Carless, 2013) because of learning unexpected events about themselves and others (Berry, 2013). Therefore, reflexivity engages autoethnographers to understand "both text and context, as it relates not just to the isolated experience of the teller or ethnographer, but to communities and cultures of thought which may be sutured to the auto/ethnographer's experience or lifescript" (Alexander, 2011, p. 105).

Cyberethnography: Documenting Life Online

December 3, 2010. Visiting Bahay Tsinoy was an enlightening experience for me to learn about the (trans)national nature of Tsina/oy identity. I would not have thought there is a dedicated space in the heart of the city documenting the history of Tsina/oys. I am grateful to have witnessed different eras that reminded me of the past and present. Visiting Bahay Tsinoy made me feel at home for reflecting my (trans)national hybrid experiences and enabling me to be reflexive of my personal and cultural identities.

Besides visiting Bahay Tsinoy, coming home to Manila to conduct (auto) ethnographic research has given me opportunities to examine Tsina/oy identity from another perspective. However, I remind myself that the reason I am writing about Tsina/oy identity was a result of finding Tsinoy.com. I can't believe it has been a few years since the first time I found this Tsina/oy community online. I did not think initially that Tsinoy.com would turn into a research project. While living in Carbondale, Illinois to attend graduate school, I discovered Tsinoy.com as a point of reconnecting with my own Tsinoy identity and community. However, after reading plenty of rich discussions on Tsinoy.com, I became convinced that I needed to know more about the (re)making of Tsina/oy identity in a (trans)national online space.

I conducted a cyberethnography of Tsinoy.com for eight months (February 19, 2007–October 24, 2007) by visiting and collecting data on the Web site at least three times a week for the intent of (re)connecting with my Tsinoyness while also learning about hybridity in a (trans)national online community. Ethnographies conducted online have been considered as the following: online ethnography, virtual ethnography, digital ethnography, netnography, cyberethnography, among others (Lester, 2020). I chose to use cyberethnography because it focuses on the "cyberspace, a view that emphasized the internet as cultural spaces in which meaningful human interactions occur" (Markham, 2018, p. 1139). Moreover, cyberspace is a where "we form and cultivate communities" to find a sense of belonging (Atay, 2020, p. 269). Focusing on communities established online, cyberethnographers observe, interact, and converse with online participants to analyze email lists, discussion forums, chat rooms, and Multi-User Dungeons (MUDs) (Markham, 1998; Ward, 1999).

Historically, cyberethnography emerged in the mid-1990s (Robinson & Schulz, 2009, 2011). At this time, much of cyberethnographic research focused on tech-savvy populations and gamers that treated "their online identities and interactions as a kind of 'play' or 'game'" (Robinson & Schulz, 2009, p. 687) to present a different version of themselves and impersonate fictional characters or other participants (Stone, 1995). Because of these online sites and their "near-total anonymity," "participants could create and sustain whatever self-presentations their online interlocutors would accept as genuine within the confines of that particular online interactional space" (Robinson & Schulz, 2011, pp. 181–182). By the end of 1990s, cyberethnographers began recognizing that online participants are not merely presenting a different version of themselves but engaging in blurred performances of online and offline identities (Garcia et al., 2009; Kendall, 2002; Markham, 1998). Even though most cyberethnographies have focused on online participants interacting entirely through written texts (Turner, 2002) as ethnographic evidence (Gajjala, 2013), recent ethnographies online have become multimodal in nature where image, video, and sound could be present simultaneously as sites of investigation (Robinson & Schulz, 2009).

Given the complexity of cyberspace, the cyberethnographer needs to be familiar with the online site's communication and technological modes as preparation for research (Garcia et al., 2009). If online community members also communicate in offline spaces, cyberethnographers may need to conduct online and offline ethnographies (Baym, 2000). Gaining access to the online field and recruiting participants require cyberethnographers' cultural knowledge of the online community under ethnographic examination (Walstrom, 2004). To do so, cyberethnographers may consider participating in the online community's activities before conducting research (Cherny, 1999). Alternatively, cyberethnographers could identify as a member or a supporter of the community (LeBesco, 2004). Regardless of their cultural knowledge and experience, cyberethnographers have an ethical responsibility to ask permission to study an online community (Lane, 2016). Murthy (2011) adds that cyberethnographers must also post a message informing members about their research and researcher identity (Robinson & Schulz, 2011). In my case, I posted a message on Tsinoy.com introducing myself as a Tsinoy researcher studying the performance and negotiation of Tsina/oy identity. Thus, Tsinoy.com forum members knew me as a Tsinoy researcher and was aware of my intent to observe and participate online.

Because digital data are considered public texts, many ethics boards feel it is unnecessary to ask online participants for research consent (Markham, 2006). As Lester (2020) notes, "Gaining consent online has been frequently described as complex and problematic, particularly in spaces wherein anonymity is a built-in feature of the space (e.g., chatrooms where participants use fake user names)" (p. 418). Due to the nature of the Internet research and considering Lester (2020) and Marham's (2006) points, I did not require each participant to return a signed consent form. Instead, I posted a message asking members who did not wish to participate in my research to email me directly. As for those members who agreed to share their experiences, I used pseudonyms in place of existing screen names to protect their online identities.

After providing information about the research, it is essential for cyberethnographers to understand the process of engaging in participant observation online. Cyberethnographers can engage in "lurking" or "unobtrusive observation" (Garcia et al., 2009, p. 58) to gain information about the community (Kozinets & Handelman, 1998; Shoham, 2004). Beyond lurking, "observation in online research involves watching text and images on a screen" (Garcia et al., 2009, p. 58). More specifically, participant observation in cyberspaces can be performed by investigating emails, chat rooms, Web sites, instant messaging, among others (Garcia et al., 2009). Even though Tsinoy.com had several discussion forums concerning popular culture, food, and cultural/linguistic practices, I chose to examine the discussion forum, *"Tsinoy Nga!"* ("Tsinoy Really!"), because Tsina/oys who participated in this forum specifically talked about Tsina/oy identity and linguistic and cultural practices (Hao, 2013).

Besides examining textual and visual materials, engaging in dialogue with online participants is still paramount to ethnographic research (Bell, 2001), which can be accomplished by conducting either or both online and offline interviews (Garcia et al., 2009). Online interviews are normally performed asynchronously using email and discussion boards, but synchronous online channels like instant messaging and chat are also common. Recent technological advances also make it possible to use videoconferencing as another means to conduct synchronous online interviews (Fetterman, 2002). Depending on the nature of the research, offline interviews may be used to verify identities and information in cyberspace (Turkle, 1995), bridge gaps found in online data (Leung, 2005), and accommodate online participants' preferences (Garcia et al., 2009). As part of my ethnographic evidence while on Tsinoy.com, I posted questions and responded to discussions in the forum. For example, I asked what "Tsina/oy" means to Tsinoy.com members and how they identify culturally. Further, I observed their performance of Tsina/oyness online based on discussions about linguistic and cultural practices. Because Tsinoy.com members came from all over the world, I was also interested in the different tensions they faced as (trans)national Tsina/oys.

While interacting with online participants, cyberethnographers must also take into account their reflexivity, which "implies theorizing and analyzing how subjectivities of the researcher and the subjects get mutually constituted in the interaction" (Rybas & Gajjala, 2007, Cyberethnography section, para. 7). Since it is difficult to distinguish between private and public identity performances in online communities (Catterall & Maclaran, 2002; Robinson & Schulz, 2011), "various categories such as public/private, audience/author, producer/consumer, and text/human subject" are blurred (Gajjala, 2004, p. 34). Therefore, participants could "talk back" in order to question and challenge the researcher's authority and "conceptual and methodological assumptions" (p. 31). As Gajjala

(2004) explains, "Considering the interactive nature of online participation, questions arise as to who is an ethnographer, who qualifies to be a 'native' informant, and what the options are for refusing to be a subject" (p. 29). Moreover, cyberethnographers must engage in reflexivity by acknowledging virtual communities are "imbedded in real-life communities" (p. 19) where certain discourses are privileged while others are marginalized or silenced.

Representing collected textual data in cyberspace is another important point of consideration. Like Markham (1998), I made minor changes to grammar and spelling (if needed) to aid in comprehension of participants' messages. If online participants did not indicate their gender in the forum, I used "they" or "them" for pronouns in this book. Additionally, it is worth noting that I retained the members' online messages written in Tagalog and Hokkien with accompanied English translations to maintain Tsina/oy experiences as they appeared online.

(Auto)Ethnographically Tsina/oys

December 3, 2010. I did not think my cyberethnography of Tsinoy.com would have led me to doing ethnographic interviews in Manila a few years later. Even though I learned so much as a cyberethnographer on Tsinoy.com, I wanted to come home to Manila to (re)discover what it means to be Tsinoy. Reuniting with family in Manila has reminded me a part of myself. Staying with my grandmother and aunt, I am reliving some of my childhood memories by reminiscing about family gatherings and cultural practices that helped shape my Tsinoyness. While my experiences helped me understand who I am, I believe engaging in a multimethodological ethnographic project would allow me to learn about Tsina/oyness from a (trans)national perspective. Through critical ethnographic interview, autoethnography, and cyberethnography, the subsequent chapters will shed light on the multiple realities of Tsina/oys in both physical and online spaces to conceptualize what makes me and other Tsina/oys (trans)national hybrids.

Speaking with Denisa and Vivian a couple of days ago has reassured me that my research matters. Denisa and Vivian welcomed me into their storied lives—lives filled with rich experiences of the past and present. More importantly, the opportunity to converse with them has prompted me to consider intersectionality and reflexivity by making a conscious effort to identify the similarities and differences among Tsina/oy participants. As I continue to stay in Manila for the next couple of weeks, I look forward to meeting other Tsina/oys to find out their own realities of performing hybridity in everyday life.

References

Adams, T. E. (2017). Autoethnographic responsibilities. *International Review of Qualitative Research, 10*(1), 62–66. https://doi.org/10.1525/irqr.2017.10.1.62

Adams, T. E., Ellis, C., & Holman Jones, S. (2017). Autoethnography. In J. Matthes, C. Davis, & R. F. Potter (Eds.), *The international encyclopedia of communication research methods* (pp. 1–11). Wiley-Blackwell. https://doi.org/10.1002/9781118901731.iecrm0011

Alcoff, L. M. (1991). The problem of speaking for others. *Cultural Critique, 20*, 5–32. https://doi.org/10.2307/1354221

Alexander, B. K. (1999). Performing culture in the classroom: An instructional (auto)ethnography. *Text and Performance Quarterly, 19*(4), 307–331. https://doi.org/10.1080/10462939909366272

Alexander, B. K. (2006). *Performing black masculinity: Race, culture, and queer identity*. AltaMira Press.

Alexander, B. K. (2011). Standing in the wake: A critical auto/ethnographic exercise on reflexivity in three movements. *Cultural StudiesCritical Methodologies, 11*(2), 98–107. https://doi.org/10.1177/1532708611401328

Alexander, B. K. (2021). Critical autoethnography as intersectional praxis: A performative pedagogical interplay on bleeding borders of identity. In R. M. Boylorn & M. P. Orbe (Eds.), *Critical autoethnography: Intersecting cultural identities in everyday life* (2nd ed., pp. 32–44). Routledge.

Atay, A. (2020). What is cyber or digital autoethnography? *International Review of Qualitative Research, 13*(3), 267–279. https://doi.org/10.1177/1940844720934373

Banks, S. P., & Banks, A. (2000). Reading "The Critical Life": Autoethnography as pedagogy. *Communication Education, 49*(3), 233–238. https://doi.org/10.1080/03634520009379212

Baym, N. K. (2000). *Tune in, log on: Soaps, fandom, and online community*. SAGE.

Bell, D. (2001). *An introduction to cyberculture*. Routledge.

Berry, K. (2013). Spinning autoethnographic reflexivity, cultural critique, and negotiating selves. In S. Holman Jones, T. E. Adams, & C. Ellis (Eds.), *Handbook of autoethnography* (pp. 209–227). Left Coast Press.

Berry, K. (2016). *Bullied: Tales of torment, identity, and youth*. Routledge.

Boylorn, R. M. (2011). Gray or for colored girls who are tired of chasing rainbows: Race and reflexivity. *Cultural Studies ↔ Critical Methodologies, 11*(2), 178–186. https://doi.org/10.1177/1532708611401336

Boylorn, R. M. (2012). *Sweetwater: Black woman and narratives of resilience*. Left Coast Press.

Boylorn, R. M. (2014). A story & a stereotype: An angry and strong auto/ethnography of race, class, and gender. In R. M. Boylorn & M. P. Orbe (Eds.), *Critical autoethnography: Intersecting cultural identities in everyday life* (pp. 129–143). Left Coast Press.

Boylorn, R. M., & Orbe, M. P. (Eds.). (2014). *Critical autoethnography: Intersecting cultural identities in everyday life*. Left Coast Press.

Boylorn, R. M., & Orbe, M. P. (Eds.). (2021). *Critical autoethnography: Intersecting cultural identities in everyday life* (2nd ed.). Routledge.

Calafell, B. M. (2007). *Latina/o communication studies: Theorizing performance*. Peter Lang.

Calafell, B. M. (2013). (I)dentities: Considering accountability, reflexivity, and intersectionality in the I and the we. *Liminalities: A Journal of Performance Studies, 9*(2), 6–13. http://liminalities.net/9-2/calafell.pdf

Calafell, B. M., Eguchi, S., & Abdi, S. (2020). Introduction: *De-Whitening intersectionality in intercultural communication*. In S. Eguchi, B. M. Calafell, & S. Abdi (Eds.), *De-Whitening intersectionality: Race, intercultural communication, and politics* (pp. xvii–xxvii). Lexington Books.

Carspecken, P. F. (1996). *Critical ethnography in educational research. A theoretical and practical guide*. Routledge.

Catterall, M., & Maclaran, P. (2002). Researching consumers in virtual worlds: A cyberspace odyssey. *Journal of Consumer Behavior, 1*(3), 228–237. https://doi.org/10.1002/cb.68

Chang, H. (2008). *Autoethnography as method*. Left Coast Press.

Chawla, D. (2013). Walk, walking, talking, home. In S. Holman Jones, T. E. Adams, & C. Ellis (Eds.), *Handbook of autoethnography* (pp. 162–172). Left Coast Press.

Chawla, D., & Atay, A. (2018). Introduction: Decolonizing autoethnography. *Cultural Studies ↔ Critical Methodologies, 18*(1), 3–8. https://doi.org/10.1177/1532708617728955

Cherny, L. (1999). *Conversation and community: Chat in a virtual world*. CSLI Publications.

Church, K. (1995). *Forbidden narratives: Critical autobiography as social science*. Gordon and Breach.

Conquergood, D. (1982). Performing as a moral act. Ethical dimensions of the ethnography of performance. *Literature in Performance, 5*(2), 1–13. https://doi.org/10.1080/10462938509391578

Conquergood, D. (1991). Rethinking ethnography: Cultural politics and rhetorical strategies. *Communication Monographs, 58*(2), 179–194. https://doi.org/10.1080/03637759109376222

Conquergood, D. (2002). Performance studies: Interventions and radical research. *The Drama Review, 46*(2), 145–156. http://www.jstor.org/stable/1146965

Cresswell, J. W. (2007). *Qualitative inquiry & research design: Choosing among five approaches* (2nd ed.). SAGE.

Deitering, A. (2017). Introduction: Why autoethnography? In A. Deitering, R. Schroeder, & R. Stoddart (Eds.), *The Self as subject: Autoethnographic research into identity, culture, and academic librarianship* (pp. 1–22). American Library Association.

Douglas, K., & Carless, D. (2013). A history of autoethnographic inquiry. In S. Holman Jones, T. E. Adams, & C. Ellis (Eds.), *Handbook of Autoethnography* (pp. 84–106). Left Coast Press.

Dutta, M., & Basu, A. (2013). Negotiating our postcolonial selves from the ground to the ivory tower. In S. Holman Jones, T. E. Adams, & C. Ellis (Eds.), *Handbook of autoethnography* (pp. 143–161). Routledge.

Eguchi, S. (2015). Queer intercultural relationality: An autoethnography of Asian-Black (dis) connections in White gay America. *Journal of International and Intercultural Communication*, 8(1), 27–43. https://doi.org/10.1080/17513057.2015.991077

Ellis, C. (1995). *Final negotiations: A story of love, loss, and chronic illness*. Temple University Press.

Ellis, C. (2004). *The ethnographic I: A methodological novel about autoethnography*. AltaMira Press.

Ellis, C. (2009). *Revision: Autoethnographic reflections on life and work*. Left Coast Press.

Ellis, C., Adams, T. E., & Bochner, A. P. (2011). Autoethnography: An overview. *Historical Social Research*, 36(4), 273–290. https://doi.org/10.12759/hsr.36.2011.4.273-290

Ellis, C., & Bochner, A. (2000). Autoethnography, personal narrative and reflexivity. In N. Denzin & Y. Lincoln (Eds.), *The handbook of qualitative research* (2nd ed., pp. 733–768). SAGE.

Ellis, C., & Flaherty, M. G. (Eds.). (1992). *Investigating subjectivity: Research on lived experience*. SAGE.

Fassett, D. L, & Warren, J. T. (2007). *Critical communication pedagogy*. SAGE.

Fetterman, D. M. (2002). Web surveys to digital movies: Technological tools of the trade. *Educational Researcher*, 31(6), 29–38. https://doi.org/10.3102/0013189X031006029

Gajjala, R. (2004). *Cyber selves: Feminist ethnographies of South Asian women*. AltaMira Press.

Gajjala, R. (2013). Always at crossroads: Studying online/offline intersections as a postcolonial feminist researcher. In A. N. Valdivia (Ed.), *The international encyclopedia of media studies* (pp. 1–17). Blackwell. https://doi.org/10.1002/9781444361506.wbiems100

Garcia, A. C., Standlee, A., Bechkoff, J., & Cui, Y. (2009). Ethnographic approaches to the internet and computer-mediated communication. *Journal of Contemporary Ethnography*, 38(1), 52–84. https://doi.org/10.1177/0891241607310839

Glesne, C. (1999). *Becoming qualitative researchers: An introduction*. New York: Routledge.

Goldschmidt, W. (1977). Anthropology and the coming crisis: An autoethnographic appraisal. *American Anthropologist*, 79(2), 293–308. https://doi.org/10.1525/aa.1977.79.2.02a00060

Goltz, D. B. (2011). Frustrating the "I": Critical dialogic reflexivity with personal voice. *Text and Performance Quarterly*, 31(4), 386–405. https://doi.org/10.1080/10462937.2011.602707

Greenspan, H. (1998). *On listening to Holocaust survivors: Recounting and life history*. Praeger.

Griffin, R. A. (2012). "I am an angry black woman": Black feminist autoethnography, voice, and resistance. *Women's Studies in Communication*, 35(2), 138–157. https://doi.org/10.1080/07491409.2012.724524

Hammersley, M. (1990). *Reading ethnographic research: A critical guide*. Longman.

Hammersley, M., & Atkinson, P. (1995). *Ethnography: Principles in practice* (2nd ed.). Routledge.

Hao, R. N. (2013). Virtually Tsina/oy: Performing and negotiating diasporic hybridity online. *Qualitative Communication Research*, 2(2), 159–181. https://doi.org/10.1525/qcr.2013.2.2.159

Hao, R. N. (2021). Performing fortune cookie: An autoethnographic performance on diasporic hybridity. In R. M. Boylorn & M. P. Orbe (Eds.), *Critical autoethnography: Intersecting cultural identities in everyday life* (2nd ed., pp. 45–56). Routledge.

Hayano, D. M. (1979). Auto-ethnography: Paradigms, problems, and prospects. *Human Organization*, 38(1), 99–104.

Heider, K. G. (1975). What do people do? Dani auto-ethnography. *Journal of Anthropological Research, 31*(1), 3–17. https://doi.org/10.1086/jar.31.1.3629504

Holman Jones, S. (2005). Autoethnography: Making the personal political. In N. K. Denzin & Y. S. Lincoln (Eds.), *Handbook of qualitative research* (3rd ed., pp. 763–791). SAGE.

Holman Jones, S. (2018). Creative selves/creative cultures: Critical autoethnography, performance, and pedagogy. In S. Holman Jones & M. Pruyn (Eds.), *Creative selves/creative cultures: Critical autoethnography, performance, and pedagogy* (pp. 3–20). Palgrave Macmillan.

Holman Jones, S., & Adams, T. E. (2010). Autoethnography as a queer method. In K. Browne & C. J. Nash (Eds.), *Queer methods and methodologies: Intersecting queer theories and social science research* (pp. 195–214). New York, NY: Routledge.

hooks, b. (1994). Homeplace: A site of resistance. In D. S. Madison (Ed.), *The woman that I am: The literature and culture of contemporary women of color* (pp. 448-454). St. Martin's.

Jones, R. G., Jr. (2010). Putting privilege into practice through "intersectional reflexivity": Ruminations, interventions, and possibilities. *Reflections: Narratives of Professional Helping, 16*, 122–125.

Kendall, L. (2002). *Hanging out in the virtual pub: Masculinities and relationships online*. University of California Press.

Kinchloe, L. J., & McLaren, P. (2000). Rethinking critical theory and qualitative research. In N. K. Denzin & Y. S. Lincoln (Eds.), *Handbook of qualitative research* (2nd ed., pp. 279–313). SAGE.

Kozinets, R. V., & Handelman, J. (1998). Ensouling consumption: A netnographic exploration of the meaning of boycotting behavior. *Advances in Consumer Research, 25*(1), 475–480.

Lane, J. (2016). The digital street: An ethnographic study of networked street life in Harlem. *American Behavioral Scientist, 60*(1), 43–58. https://doi.org/10.1177/0002764215601711

LeBesco, K. (2004). Managing visibility, intimacy, and focus in online critical ethnography. In M. D. Johns, S.–L. S. Chen, & G. J. Hall (Eds.), *Online social research: Methods, issues, and ethics* (pp. 63–79). Peter Lang.

Lester, J. N. (2020). Going digital in ethnography: Navigating the ethical tensions and productive possibilities. *Cultural Studies ↔ Critical Methodologies, 20*(5), 414–424. https://doi.org/10.1177/1532708620936995

Leung, L. (2005). *Virtual ethnicity: Race, resistance and the World Wide Web*. Ashgate Publishing Company.

Levinson, B. A., & Holland, D. (1996). The cultural production of the educated person: An introduction. In B. A. Levinson, D. E. Foley, & D. Holland (Eds.), *The cultural production of the educated person: Critical ethnographies of schooling and local practice* (pp. 1–56). State University of New York Press.

Lionnet, F. (1989). *Autobiographical voices: Race, gender, self-portraiture*. Cornell University Press.

MacGowan, J. (1883). *English and Chinese dictionary of the Amoy dialect*. A. A. Marcal.

Madison, D. S. (2005). *Critical ethnography: Method, ethics, and performance*. SAGE.

Marcus, G. E., & Fischer, M. M. J. (1986). *Anthropology as cultural critique: An experimental moment in the human sciences*. University of Chicago Press.

Markham, A. N. (1998). *Life online: Researching real experience in virtual space*. AltaMira Press.

Markham, A. N. (2006). Method as ethic, ethic as method. *Journal of Information Ethics*, 15(2), 37–55.

Markham, A. N. (2018). Ethnography in the digital internet era: From fields to flows, descriptions to interventions. In N. K. Denzin & Y. S. Lincoln (Eds.), *The SAGE handbook of qualitative research* (5th ed., pp. 1129–1162). SAGE.

Mattson, M., & Stage, C. W. (2003). Contextualized conversation: Interviewing exemplars. In R. P. Clair (Ed.), *Expressions of ethnography: Novel approaches to qualitative methods* (pp. 107–118). State University of New York Press.

McIntosh, D. M. D., & Eguchi, S. (2020). The troubled past, present disjuncture, and possible futures: Intercultural performance communication. *Journal of Intercultural Communication Research*, 49(5), 395–409. https://doi.org/10.1080/17475759.2020.1811996

Meyerhoff, B. (1981). Life history among the elderly: Performance, visibility, and re-membering. In J. Ruby (Ed.), *A crack in the mirror: Reflexive perspectives in anthropology* (pp. 99–117). University of Pennsylvania Press.

Murthy, D. (2011). Emergent digital ethnographic methods for social research. In S. N. Hesse-Biber (Ed.), *The handbook of emergent technologies in social research* (pp. 158–179). Oxford University Press.

Noblit, G. W., Flores, S. Y., & Murillo, E. G. (2004). *Postcritical ethnography: Reinscribing critique*. Cress, NJ: Hampton Press.

Pathak, A. (2013). Musings on postcolonial autoethnography. In S. Holman Jones, T. E. Adams, & C. Ellis (Eds.), *Handbook of autoethnography* (pp. 595–608). Routledge.

Pensoneau-Conway, S. L., & Toyosaki, S. (2011). Automethodology: Tracing a home for praxis-oriented ethnography. *International Journal of Qualitative Methods*, 10(4), 378–399. https://doi.org/10.1177/160940691101000406

Reed-Danahay, D. E. (Ed.). (1997). *Auto/ethnography. Rewriting the self and the social*. Berg.

Robinson, L., & Schulz, J. (2009). New avenues for sociological inquiry: Evolving forms of ethnographic practice. *Sociology*, 43(4), 685–698. https://doi.org/10.1177/0038038509105415

Robinson, L., & Schulz, J. (2011). New Fieldsites, new methods: New ethnographic opportunities. In S. N. Hesse-Biber (Ed.), *The Handbook of emergent technologies in social research* (pp. 180–198). Oxford University Press.

Rubin, H. J., & Rubin, I. S. (1995). *Qualitative interviewing: The art of hearing data*. SAGE.

Rybas, N., & Gajjala, R. (2007). Developing cyberethnographic research methods for understanding digitally mediated identities. *Forum: Qualitative Social Research*, 8(3). Retrieved from https://www.qualitative-research.net/index.php/fqs/article/view/282/619

Shoham, A. (2004). Flow experiences and image making: An online chat-room ethnography. *Psychology and Marketing*, 21(10), 855–882. https://doi.org/10.1002/mar.20032

Simon, R. I., & Dippo, D. (1986). On critical ethnographic work. *Anthropology & Education Quarterly*, 17(4), 195–202. http://www.jstor.org/stable/3216428

Spieldenner, A. R., & Eguchi, S. (2020). Different sameness: Queer autoethnography and coalition politics. *Cultural Studies ↔ Critical Methodologies*, 20(2), 134–143. https://doi.org/10.1177/1532708619884962

Spradley, J. P. (1979). *The ethnographic interview*. Harcourt Brace Jovanovich.

Stage, C. W., & Mattson, M. (2003). Ethnographic interviewing as contextualized conversation. In R. P. Clair (Ed.), *Expressions of ethnography: Novel approaches to qualitative methods* (pp. 97–105). State University of New York Press.

Stone, A. R. (1995). *The war of desire and technology.* MIT Press.

Thomas, J. (1993). *Doing critical ethnography.* SAGE.

Thomas, J. (2003). Musings on critical ethnography, meanings, and symbolic violence. In R. P. Clair (Ed.), *Expressions of ethnography: Novel approaches to qualitative methods* (pp. 45–54). State University of New York Press.

Toyosaki, S. (2018). Toward de/postcolonial autoethnography: Critical relationality with the academic second persona. *Cultural Studies ↔ Critical Methodologies, 18*(1), 32–42. https://doi.org/10.1177/1532708617735133

Trinh, M. (1989). *Woman, native, other: Writing postcoloniality and feminism.* Indiana University Press.

Turkle, S. (1995). *Life on the screen: Identity in the Age of the Internet.* Simon & Schuster.

Turner, J. (2002). *Face to face.* Stanford University Press.

Van Maanen, J. (1988). *Tales of the field: On writing ethnography.* University of Chicago Press.

Villenas, S., & Foley, D. (2002). Chicano/Latino critical ethnography of education: Borderlands cultural productions from La Frontera. In R. R. Valencia (Ed.), *Chicano school failure and success: Past, present, and future* (2nd ed., pp. 195–226). Routledge Falmer.

Walstrom, M. K. (2004). Ethics and engagement in communication scholarship: Analyzing public, online support groups as researcher/participant-experiencer. In E. A. Buchanan (Ed.), *Virtual research ethics: Issues and controversies* (pp. 174–202). Information Science Publishing.

Ward, K. (1999). Cyber-ethnography and the emergence of the virtually new community. *Journal of Information Technology, 14*(1), 95–105. https://doi.org/10.1177/026839629901400108

PERFORMING TSINA/OYNESS: (E)MERGING CHINESE AND FILIPINA/O IDENTITIES

December 8, 2010. I am getting ready to meet with two Tsinoy participants, Eric and Mike, at Starbucks, which is conveniently located a couple of blocks from my grandmother and aunt's apartment. Standing on a corner adjacent to the Seattle-based coffee shop, there is still a heavy presence of cars and jeepneys past dinner time. Trying to cross the street without a crosswalk and stop light, I am depending on my street smarts to get to my destination as safely as possible. Holding up my hand as a signal for cars and jeepneys to slow down, I trek along the street in the midst of moving vehicles in both directions. I finally arrive at the familiar coffee chain that reminds me of home in the United States. The coffee shop's ambiance reflects the Christmas season with its bright lighting and décor. Occupied only by a handful of people at this hour, I locate Eric and Mike sitting by the window. I greet and converse with them briefly. Insisting I treat Eric and Mike for their beverage of choice, we take some time to enjoy our iced drinks before starting the interview.

Eric and Mike were two of the 32 voices who shared their experiences on what it means to be "Tsina/oy." The critical ethnographic interviews were conducted in Manila and surrounding cities in December 2010 and June 2011. Recognizing my privileges as a (trans)national Tsinoy researcher from the United States, I utilize Critical Intercultural Performance (CIP) to remind me of the significance of intersectionality and reflexivity for analyzing diverse Tsina/oy experiences (Hao, 2020). My critical ethnographic interview analysis begins with Tsina/oy participants' conceptualization of "Tsina/oy" as an identity label. Second, focusing on the intersectionality of national, ethnic, and class identities, I investigate Tsina/oy participants' embodiment of their Chinese and Filipina/o identities as (trans)national hybridity. Finally, I discuss Tsina/oy participants' negotiation of multiple tensions in different cultural and social contexts.

What's in a Name?: (Re)Defining "Tsina/oy"

Kaisa (also known as *Kaisa para sa Kaunlaran*, which means "Unity in Progress") is a Chinese Filipina/o organization responsible for coining "Tsinoy" in 1992 (Uytanlet, 2016). Combining "Tsino" (Chinese) and "Pinoy" (colloquial for Filipino) results in a hybrid identity of "Tsinoy" (Yap, 2018). Additionally, "Tsinoy" was established to distinguish local-born Filipina/os who are of Chinese descent from recent Chinese immigrants (Uytanlet, 2016). Even though many Tsina/oy participants found "Tsina/oy" an appropriate term to describe their Chinese and Filipina/o identities, some had a different understanding of what it means. Because of its complexity, "Tsina/oy" can be defined in a variety of ways culturally, socially, and politically. In the context of my analysis, I consider "Tsina/oy" as a performance of culture based on the participants' embodiment of Chinese and Filipina/o traditions and practices. Tsina/oys can also perform their hybridity through social interactions with other Tsina/oys and Filipina/os. Furthermore, as a political identity, I argue that "Tsina/oy" can be communicated to (re)claim the hybridity of Chinese and Filipina/o identities.

Consistent with *Kaisa*'s definition, all 32 participants agreed that "Tsina/oy" represents the hybridity of Chinese and Filipina/o identities. However, participants' responses varied in terms of their conceptualization of "Tsina/oy." Many participants like Dan, Ethel, Greg, Tina, and Wesley considered Tsina/oys as "Chinese Filipina/o," which reflected Emilio's definition of "Filipinos of Chinese descent." Therefore, it is not surprising that Dino, Eric, Laura, Leslie, Martha, and Vivian categorized "Tsina/oys" as Chinese who were born or raised in the Philippines. By contrast, some participants like Denisa and Rita referred to "Tsina/oys" as "Filipino Chinese." Because "Tsina/oy" can be associated with "Chinese Filipina/o" and "Filipina/o Chinese," it is imperative to understand the distinction between them. "Chinese Filipino" as a term was popularized in the 1980s "to refer to locally born Chinese who grew up and were educated in the Philippines, whose hearts and minds are Filipino but who traced their cultural origins to China" (Guillermo, 2012, p. 443). "Chinese Filipina/o," therefore, communicates the hybridity of Chinese ancestry and Filipina/o culture based on established national, institutional, and local practices.

Supporting Guillermo's (2012) definition, Anson also provided his own experience that would help distinguish "Chinese Filipina/o" from "Filipina/o Chinese." Anson said the following:

> Chinese Filipino...so, you state, "I'm Filipino, but with Chinese heritage." So, Filipino Chinese, if you reverse it, would mean a totally different thing. Most of my father and most of us...it's not a choice. We've been Chinese all through our staying in the Philippines because there's no naturalization law until 1975. If the naturalization was introduced to us in the [19]60s, we could have been Filipinos even that early. It took us a long time. That's on papers, but on the mindset, we're Filipinos almost entire our lifetime.

Born in Hong Kong but raised in the Philippines, Anson explained why many Tsina/oys have struggled with their hybridity culturally and politically. Recounting from his father's and other Tsina/oys' experience, it took a long time for Tsina/oys to be granted Filipina/o citizenship, especially since many of them were born and/or raised in the Philippines. As a result, many older Tsina/oys today tend to be thought of only as Chinese, even though a part of them has always been Filipina/o. Perhaps it could be explained why some Tsina/oys like Denisa and Rita would identify as "Filipina/o Chinese" to display publicly of who they are in the land of their birth or the place they have always called home. As See (1997a) notes, the etymology of "Filipino Chinese" was used during the height of the Filipinization policies of the Philippine government after gaining its independence in 1946, which resulted in "legislative measures such as the nationalization of retail trade" (p. 43) and nationalization of professions (e.g., engineering, architecture, and medicine) that barred the Chinese from engaging in a variety of economic and professional activities (Tan, 1988). As a response, many ethnic Chinese applied for Filipina/o citizenship (Guillermo, 2012).

As the Chinese continue to be integrated in Philippine life, many of them today embody both Chinese and Filipina/o cultures. Like many Tsina/oy participants, Esmeralda emphasized "Tsina/oy" as hybridity where blending of cultures occurs (e.g., Anzaldúa, 1999; Bakhtin, 1981; Bhabha, 1994; Calafell, 2004; Hao, 2021; Kraidy, 2005; Nam, 2001; Young, 2009): "Tsinoy is a mixture of Chinese and Filipino. Sometimes, it's either by blood or mixture of Chinese and Filipino cultures." Tsina/oyness can also be understood as embodying cultural practices in everyday life. Lulu spoke about "Tsina/oy" as performance of Chinese and Filipina/o cultures:

> It means Chinese born and raised in the Philippines with, uh, Filipino, um, culture-adopting Filipino customs, traditions, and, um, at times, they can still speak Chinese and others they cannot totally speak the language, but, of course, all of us have Chinese blood...You cannot be a Tsinoy like you're only speaking Tagalog; you must cling on to your Chinese traditions. To be a Tsinoy, you must blend in, but you still retain your Chinese feature—that's a Tsinoy for me.

Tsina/oy as hybridity, as outlined by Lulu, works as a collaborative process that involves conscious and unconscious performances of hybrid selves (Young, 2009), which reinforces merging of cultures. Lulu's point, however, is striking because of the specificity of a Tsina/oy as having Chinese ancestry who consciously performs both Chinese and Filipina/o cultural practices. Embodying both Chinese and Filipina/o traditions and cultural practices is an example of performative acts (Butler, 1988) that are "inscribed on the body—performed through the body—to mark identities" (Madison & Hamera, 2006, p. xviii). Because performative acts are repetitive in nature (Butler, 1990), cultural identities influence how one embodies culture through gestures, clothes, etc. (Madison & Hamera, 2006, p. xviii). To perform Tsina/oy identity, Lulu and other Tsina/oys communicated one should be able to engage in performative acts that represent both Chinese and Filipina/o cultures.

Contrary to Lulu, Rachel remarked that Tsina/oyness should not be restricted through the performance of Chinese linguistic and cultural practices. Because of hybridity and assimilation, Rachel offered the following point:

> Right now, people are mainly using Tsinoy, which is a merging of two cultures. Um, right now, most of the third-generation Chinese Filipino children are more, how do I say this, assimilated in the Filipino culture. In fact, they speak in Filipino generally or Tagalog; they can't even speak Chinese. They look Chinese, but they can't speak Chinese...When you say "Tsinoy," or when you call someone "Tsinoy," they have probably half, one-fourth, or one-half part Chinese and Filipino blood.

Confirming Rachel's point, See (1997a) states, "It is an unfortunate reality that many young Chinese have lost the facility to speak, much less to read and write, in Chinese" (p. 35). Because they lack Chinese (Hokkien) fluency, many Tsina/oys, especially younger Tsina/oys, have a broader view of hybridity without having to demonstrate a specific cultural knowledge or skill. Rachel's point touched on the younger generations' intercultural identity that straddles in-between cultural traditions and practices that (re)define who they are (Young, 2009). The intercultural identity among younger generations of Tsina/oys appears to have evolved beyond linguistic proficiency, which reinforces hybridity's "processes of transformation and resistance" (Tankei-Aminian, 2016, p. 204) by reconstructing what it means to be Tsina/oy in their respective cultural communities.

Despite the term "Tsina/oy" providing different possibilities in understanding hybridity, resistance to "Tsina/oy" could emerge due to cultural and political reasons. Mike, for example, voiced his concerns:

> Not really [I don't really like the term "Tsina/oy"]. Well, um, people, words evolve, um, words change every time, um, and then every generation or every few years people make new words to describe. Before they don't describe it as "Tsinoy." They say "Fil-Chi," and now since it changes, they use the word "Tsinoy." Some other people I heard that they use the word "PinChik"—"Pinoy Inchik" [Filipino Chinese]—but for me those, um, words ["PinChik"] they used to describe are those, are a little, um, racist and discriminative.

Mike attributed his resistance to using the term "Tsina/oy" due to the instability of identity labels that can't keep up with current cultural and political times. Before *Kaisa* coined "Tsinoy" in 1992 (Uytanlet, 2016), the Chinese in the Philippines had different identity labels: "Sangleys" (frequent visitors) during the Spanish colonial period, "Intsik" (often considered derogatory), "Pinsino" (Philippine-born Chinese), "Chinese Filipino," "Filipino Chinese," among others (See, 1997a, 1997b). With the evolution of identity labels identifying the Chinese in the Philippines, the meanings have changed historically, culturally, socially, and politically. Thus, identities are performative in nature in which they "draw on and engage historically sedimented conventions and re-encode these conventions in the process" (Mendoza et al., 2002, p. 317). From "PinChik" (derived from "Intsik") to "Fil-Chi" to "Tsinoy," Mike felt that "Tsinoy" as it is used today may be a fad because it has gained popularity, but that could very well not be used in the future. Perhaps Mike's concern can be associated with some of the terms that were introduced in the past but did not catch on with the Chinese Filipina/o population. For instance, "in the 1960s to 1970s, some sociologists and anthropologists proposed terms such as *Pinsino, Filisino,* and various combinations," but they "never took off because they sounded too contrived and anglicized" (Guillermo, 2012, p. 443, emphasis in original).

December 14, 2010. Mike provided me with another perspective of how "Tsina/oy" can be a contested term. I look forward to hearing additional voices that could further inform me of the political nature of Tsina/oy identity. Fortunately, my aunt takes me to meet another Tsinoy participant at a Chinese restaurant that serves Cantonese cuisine in the outskirts of Manila. Located in a busy business plaza, my aunt and I enter the double glass doors to find Wayne. After scanning the restaurant from side to side, my aunt spots Wayne and we walk towards him. With Wayne's infectious laugh, he extends his hand to shake mine. I shake his hand and thank him for meeting me and my aunt. I can tell right away that Wayne is full of energy and enjoys speaking with people. His enthusiasm calms my nerves as I prepare to interview him. Like a typical Chinese restaurant during dinner time, the environment is filled with external noise of people chatting and utensils clacking with bowls and plates. Despite the background noise, I pull out my digital audio recorder and set it right on top of the table facing Wayne.

Like Mike, Wayne critiqued the term "Tsina/oy"; however, his concern focused on why "Tsina/oy" as a political identity could pose a cultural hindrance to the Chinese as ethnic minorities in the Philippines:

> It's [Tsina/oy] a created term, which is okay, but I think it [Tsina/oy] is [a] Filipino citizen politically with the allegiance to the Philippines, but culturally and ethnically you're Chinese. I'm actually uncomfortable with the term only because it sounds so informal. My theory is that is not as much as integration with the Filipino culture as much as preservation of the best of Chinese culture. If we lose the Chinese culture, we all essentially become the same as other Filipinos, and that's a tragedy for both Chinese and Filipino groups. Tsinoy is more specific to the political identity and citizenship. But, in the world of globalization, there's no need for nationalism—that's my theory, ok? Nationalism is not good for minorities because you don't get to understand them [their implications].

Wayne's resistance can be stemmed from his belief that the political movement of using "Tsina/oy" is to maintain national allegiance to the Philippines without considering its potential impact on Tsina/oys' Chinese identity. In the world of globalization, Wayne argued that nationalism does not serve minorities well due to their lack of understanding of cultural history that could result in discriminatory discourses and practices. At the height of Philippine nationalism shortly after its independence in 1946, many economic policies were established to discriminate against the Chinese barring them from participating in retail, trade, and other professional opportunities in various fields (Tan, 1988). As a political response, many Chinese applied for naturalization to demonstrate their allegiance to the Philippines. Wayne's fear may have come from what took place in the past and the assumption that Tsina/oys will assimilate to the Filipina/o culture to demonstrate Philippine nationalism. However, as Shome and Hegde (2002) assert, national identity is a part of hybrids' multiple subjectivities. Furthermore, it is inevitable for us to live in a world today in which "local" and "transnational communication and affiliations" continue to shape "our understanding of 'community,' 'nation,' and 'identity'" (Madison & Hamera, 2006, p. xx). In other words, Tsina/oys' hybridity depends on both Chinese and Filipina/o identities that help develop their sense of (trans)national community in the Philippines.

Intersectional Tsina/oyness: Performance of Ethnicity, Nationality, and Class

My interview with Wayne enlightened me on how complex Tsina/oy identity is based on its historical and political roots. Many generations of Tsina/oys continue to embody both Chinese and Filipina/o identities, but they vary in their conceptualization of what makes them "Tsina/oy." Therefore, I incorporate intersectionality when analyzing Tsina/oy experiences, which is an examination of what Yep (2016) calls "vectors of difference," such as race, gender, sexuality, class, nation, and body, that construct privileged and marginalized identities simultaneously in cultural spaces (p. 86). With intersectionality in mind, I discuss in this section how Tsina/oy participants constructed Tsina/oyness in terms of ethnic, national, and class identities.

Chinese as Ethnic and Filipina/o as National Identities

Historically, institutional and governmental policies rooted in (post)colonialism have had immense effects on the development of Tsina/oy ethnic and national identities (See, 2004). Consequently, many Tsina/oys tend to classify their Chinese and Filipina/o identities as either ethnicity or nationality. Based on my conversations with Tsina/oy participants, their responses were consistent with the understanding of ethnicity as culture, language, and traditions, while nationality was referred to citizenship, birthplace, and home:

ESMERALDA: I always tell people I'm Chinese from the Philippines. If people ask, like, "What's your origin?" I always say, "I'm Chinese." What is your citizenship? I say, "I'm Filipino."

RACHEL: I'm proud to be Tsinoy. I tell my friends this: "I have Chinese blood. I'm a Filipino citizen, and I'm also Canadian by citizenship."

Esmeralda and Rachel's responses reflected many Tsina/oys' understanding of their Chinese identity as ancestry, and Filipina/o identity is linked to citizenship or nationality. According to Bernal and Knight (1993), ethnic identity indicates one's identification with and belonging to a group membership based on shared origins, history, traditions, practices, values, and behaviors. Ethnic identity, as Esmeralda pointed out, relates to one's "origin," which can be tied to ancestry. Similarly, Rachel supported the notion of Chinese identity as ancestry by tying it to "blood." Considering both uses of "origin" and "blood," Esmeralda and Rachel, respectively, established a common understanding of Chinese ancestry as part of their Tsinay identity. As Halualani (2008) explains, "ancestry," "descent," "genealogy," and "blood quantum" could be used to quantify and qualify one's affiliation with an ethnic identity (p. 18). By contrast, national identity "refers to one's legal status in relation to a nation" that is often directly related to citizenship (Martin & Nakayama, 2018, p. 112). Supporting Martin and Nakayama's (2018) point, both Esmeralda and Rachel linked their Filipina identity with citizenship.

Like many Tsina/oys who were born to Chinese immigrant parents, they predominantly practice Chinese traditions and are multilingual with fluency in both Mandarin and Hokkien. Many baby boomer Tsina/oys tend to identify as Chinese but call the Philippines home. For example, Greg remarked, "I'm more Chinese, but I love Philippines better." Greg's "love" for the Philippines is what Shi (2005) would consider as a performance of loyalty to the home country as part of identity negotiation, rather than a display, for hybrid individuals. It is not unusual for Tsina/oys who have immigrant parents to hold on to Chinese traditions but show loyalty to their country of birth. In my own experience as a Tsinoy child, I grew up in a household that emphasized celebrating many Chinese traditions while adopting local Filipina/o practices to reflect our understanding of the Philippines as home.

Because of their Chinese upbringing in a Filipina/o environment, it is common for Tsina/oys to call themselves "Chinese Filipina/o." Tina told me she identifies as "Chinese Filipino," but she also referred to her values as "Chinese," which can be attributed to her ethnic identity. By contrast, her Filipina identity is in reference to having lived in the Philippines. Tina commented:

> For me, values—Chinese *lang*, but upbringing since we live in the Philippines so *lan e* lifestyle *si hoan-á lo*, but *lan e* values *si* Chinese, and I also studied in a Chinese school [For me, my values are Chinese, but since we live in the Philippines my upbringing is Filipina. Our values are Chinese because I also studied in a Chinese school].

Tina's point emphasized her Chinese identity is rooted to the core values of what makes her practice traditions and beliefs; her Filipinaness functions as another dimension of who she is based on the home country she grew up in. Another example came from Emilio who identifies as "Tsinoy" because, according to him, "I grew up here [in the Philippines]. I studied here [in the Philippines]. I undergo military training here [in the Philippines]." Both Tina and Emilio's Filipina/o identity is directly tied to their country of residence, the Philippines. Even though hybrid bodies are often in in-between spaces, they often consider the national boundaries where they reside as home (Halualani, 2008). Within the space in which they have established as home, Tsina/oys like Tina and Emilio make a connection between the country of residence (in many cases, country of birth) to their national identity as Filipina/o.

Even though several Tsina/oy participants classified their Chineseness with ethnicity and Filipina/oness with nationality, globalization has influenced the way some of them communicated their Tsina/oyness strategically to avoid confusion, especially when traveling abroad:

JOY: When people ask me, I actually normally would say "I'm Chinese," but I would think about it, yeah, "I'm Tsinoy," but when people ask me, I usually use the term "Chinese" just to save the explanation. [When I say] "Tsinoy," [they would ask:] "So you're half-Filipino and half-Chinese?" "No, I'm pure Chinese, but born and raised here in the Philippines," so I actually use the term "Chinese" when they ask me what race I am.

WAYNE: It depends. I'm ethnic Chinese [laughs]. I also call myself "Chinese Filipino" at times. When I go abroad, I say, "I'm Chinese from the Philippines" because that's the reality. If I said, "Chinese Filipino," they're confused. To make it simple, I just say that.

Acknowledging people's unfamiliarity with "Tsina/oy," Joy and Wayne must use identity labels strategically in different situations. Otherwise, using "Tsina/oy" could reduce its meaning from a summative approach (i.e., half Chinese and half Filipina/o) (Cupach & Imahori, 1993). Without using "Tsina/oy," Joy and Wayne referred to themselves as "pure Chinese but born and raised here in the Philippines" and "Chinese from the Philippines," respectively. Joy and Wayne emphasized Chinese identity as ethnicity, but Joy's specific reference to "pure Chinese" made her "appear authentic, natural, and continuous" (Mendoza et al., 2002, p. 318) that explicitly communicated her Chinese body. By marking their Chinese ethnicity, both Joy and Wayne associated their Filipina/o national identity with their home country of the Philippines. With such a distinction between Chinese ethnicity and Filipina/o nationality, Joy and

Wayne argued that using other labels besides "Tsina/oy" would help prevent confusion over their hybrid identity.

In addition to Joy and Wayne, Carol chose "Filipino Chinese" in place of "Tsinay" based on others' perception of her identity and convenience. Carol provided a rationale for her identity preference:

> I do classify myself as Filipino Chinese. Well, the mere fact that I was born and raised in the Philippines. My passport...My nationality is Filipino, but then, um... when I was in Tokyo, I do tell people "I'm Filipino Chinese," and I never just say "I'm Chinese," or "I'm Filipino" because they look at me and say, "Oh, you don't look Filipino." Then why do you say you're Filipino, so you shouldn't...When I say, "Filipino Chinese," so it's actually for convenience purposes to avoid questions.

Carol made it clear that she wants to be as accurate as possible when communicating her hybridity; however, there is always a possibility that others could misinterpret her Tsinay identity. While Wayne found it confusing for him to use "Chinese Filipino," Carol used something close but different in meaning ("Filipino Chinese") for convenience to avoid confusion if she were to only use "Chinese" or "Filipino." As a sojourner in Tokyo for work, globalization and transnationalism have had great influence on Carol's hybridity. When working for law firms in Tokyo, Carol often had to walk a delicate balance between being true to her hybridity and using an identity label that simplifies her body as Chinese or Filipina. Instead of choosing the latter, she insisted on using "Filipino Chinese" to represent both of her identities in the presence of Japanese coworkers. In fact, globalization blurs the fixed geographical boundaries and produces "new conceptualizations of transnational identities" (Gordon, 2016, p. 231). In essence, globalization can shape Tsina/oy identity into a transnational one. Perhaps Carol's identification with "Filipino Chinese" situated herself as someone from the Philippines whose ancestry makes her Chinese. As such, "globalization is not something that occurs in opposition to the national, or is discrete from the national. Rather, the conditions and contradictions of, and within, the nation intersect with the global, and vice-versa" (Shome & Hegde, 2002, p. 174). Many Tsina/oys like Carol align with the idea that globalization should not restrict them from performing or challenging their national identity as Filipina/os; instead, it is a constant negotiation in various personal and cultural contexts. No one can succinctly provide one unified response as to what "Tsina/oy" identity is. After all, identity is a "multivested site invested in structural constraints and the new resignifiable possibilities for remaking identity and agency" (Mendoza et al., 2002, p. 320). Based on Tsina/oy participants' experiences, Tsina/oyness functions as what Hall (1990) would consider unstable and shifting hybridity based on culture, citizenship, or identity that is tied to home.

Rich and Poor: (Re)Constructing the Binary of Class Identity

December 9, 2010. I have arrived at the Federation of Filipino-Chinese Chambers of Commerce and Industry, Inc. (FCCCII) building in Binondo, Manila. The building's full name is marked clearly in silver metallic letters that can be visible from afar. Inside the double glass doors, I take the elevator to meet with Anthony, an entrepreneur and one of FCCCII's leaders. Knowing his position and influence in the Tsina/oy community, I find it intimidating to interview Anthony. However, upon entry into his office, Anthony greets me with a friendly smile, signaling his great interest in my project. After greeting and thanking him, I tell Anthony politely that I hope I am not disrupting his busy schedule. Anthony laughs loudly and assures me not to worry about time restrictions.

My interview with someone like Anthony's professional background forced me to be cognizant of the fact that I must consider class as part of the intersectional Tsina/oy identity. In fact, many Tsina/oy participants considered themselves to be economically privileged that can be categorized primarily into these groups: college graduates, young professionals, and business workers/owners in the Metro Manila area. Historically, many Tsina/oys have experienced economic success in the Philippines (Chua, 2003). However, Chinese businesspeople in the Philippines "are very visible because they are predominantly in the frontline trading business—they buy and sell. This. . .is due to historical circumstances: trading was the only venue of livelihood opened to them during colonial times" (See, 1997a, p. 33). Additionally, the Chinese do not control all business industries in the Philippines, especially in fuel, mass transportation, textile, lumber, winery, among others. More importantly, it is necessary to recognize there are Tsina/oys who live in poverty (See, 1997a). In this section I discuss how Tsina/oyness intersects with class identity, specifically exploring Tsina/oys' assumed positions of power and the binary construction of rich Tsina/oys and poor Filipina/os.

There is no doubt many Tsina/oys have enjoyed economic success in the Philippines. Because of their class privilege, it is not surprising that many people Tsina/oys meet—Filipina/os, Tsina/oys, and others—tend to assume they are in positions of power that create a hierarchical distinction between Tsina/oys and Filipina/os. Joy gave an example of what she experienced:

> I have a client that I already introduced them to my boss, who's Filipino, and all along they thought that I own the company. When I transferred to a new company, [someone asked,] "Didn't you own the company?" [I responded,] "No, you met my boss actually." They have that connotation.

Joy's remark is indicative of what many Tsina/oys have experienced, which is often associated with being in positions of power as the owner or boss of the company because of their ethnic Chinese identity. Like Joy, Rachel also shared a similar experience:

> Uh, I deal with clients, so when they see I'm Chinese, it's automatically that it's either I'm a manager or I'm pretty much the president of the company because I'm Chinese. When they talk to me—the clients, that is—they speak in a more respective tone maybe. They try to get things to get a better deal, but if they talk to someone who's my assistant, who's Filipino, they pretty much verbally harass them because they are beneath them in a way. That's one of the unspoken beliefs that people still have when you go to a company, and there's a Chinese sitting there and there's a Filipino sitting there, you think automatically the Chinese guy is the owner. It's always the case, and the Filipino is always the assistant or the receptionist or the janitor.

Rachel commented on the stereotype of Tsina/oys who are in the position of power as presidents or managers of a company. Martin and Nakayama (2018) define stereotypes as "widely held beliefs about a group of people and are a form of generalization—a way of categorizing and processing information we receive about others in our daily life" (p. 57). Stereotypes can also be positive generalizations of a group as in the case of Tsina/oys as people who are in power, which can lead to the categorization of Filipina/os as those who work in low-level positions, such as assistants, receptionists, or even janitors. On top of these stereotypes, Rachel witnessed instances of clients—regardless of ethnic identity—treating Tsina/oys better than Filipina/os in business environments. The unfortunate effect of stereotypes is the difficulty to discard such beliefs once adopted (Martin & Nakayama, 2018). Hence, stereotypical representations of Tsina/oys and Filipina/os that Rachel described are common in business interactions.

Despite Tsina/oy stereotypes, some Tsina/oy participants acknowledged that an imbalance of power does exist between Tsina/oys and Filipina/os. For instance, it is not unusual for Tsina/oys to employ housekeepers (better known as maids in the Philippines) to help with daily chores and taking care of their child(ren). Luna attested, "I feel that some Filipino Chinese still look down to the Filipinos here—some of them—because they are maids at home."

Luna's statement is worth reminding us of the inequity that exists in many Tsina/oy households where Filipina maids and nannies dominate the local domestic working industry. In fact, Filipinas make up the overwhelming number of domestic workers, including maids, globally (Parreñas, 2000). The domestication of Filipina labor can be attributed to Spanish and U.S. colonialism that has perpetuated the "patriarchal logic that governs an unequal division of household labor" (Lan, 2003, p. 191). Consequently, Filipina women have historically been susceptible to work in the domestic industry in and beyond the Philippines.

Narrating and challenging the binary representation of Tsina/oys as affluent and Filipina/os as poor is another issue that intersects with ethnicity and class. Carol, Denisa, and Tanya opened up about the following:

CAROL: Generalizations like there's a lot of Filipinos still say "Oh, because just he or she is Filipino Chinese, that's why he or she must be rich."

DENISA: In everyday life they may say "*Napaka yaman siya*" ["She's super rich"]. There's a perception that the Chinese are all rich, they can afford to give more, and if you ask them more [money] they just get angry.

TANYA: In college, they [Filipina/os] would expect the Chinese Filipinos to be better off, to be well off, so they cannot believe that, um, I was [a] working student throughout my four years [in college]. I had to maintain a scholarship, or I cannot go to college at all, so it's more on, uh, stereotyping the Chinese.

Contrary to the stereotype of Tsina/oys as affluent, which Carol and Denisa problematized, Cariño (2001) claims that economically privileged Filipina/os also own some of the biggest companies in the Philippines. Tanya took a step further to emphasize her working class background as a Tsinay who depended on a college scholarship. Altogether, Carol, Denisa, and Tanya resisted the binary of Tsina/oys as affluent and Filipina/os as poor by seeking alternatives to and possibilities (hooks, 1990) in representing diverse Tsina/oy experiences.

The stereotype of Tsina/oys as affluent can also be demystified with Dan's personal account. As a student, Dan took jeepney (jeep), which is a type of converted bus, as public transportation to and from school. Dan explained:

Yeah, um, when I used to study in high school, I used to come into school by jeep, and the jeep stops pretty far from school, so you have to walk. Along that, you will be passing a number of universities and schools, which are generally all-Filipino schools. As a Chinese person, it's pretty common to hear people call you names as you're passing by. Um, they [Filipina/os] will call you "*Intsik beho*" [often considered an ethnic derogatory term for the Chinese (Uytanlet, 2016)].

Unlike the popular belief that all Tsina/oys have fancy cars and houses, Dan shared that some Tsina/oys rely on public transportation like jeeps, which are the cheapest form of public transportation in the Philippines (Bautista & Lema, 2018). Riding a jeep was challenging for Dan because he often heard ethnic slurs used against him. Being called *"Intsik beho"* for his Tsinoy body, Dan testified that prejudice against Tsina/oys does happen in public.

Because Tsina/oys are often stereotyped as affluent, they could engage in performances of masking their class identity so their Filipina/o peers would perceive them positively. Laura and Dan disclosed with me how they have engaged in these performances:

LAURA: With Filipinos, you have to tone down a little bit….I don't know maybe, for example, we're not the same social status, so I have to tone down so that, um, I will not offend her [Filipina] or something, and, um, when there are some Filipinos [who] are [from] economically better background, but still, I cannot expose so much of my culture to her. Maybe she will be overwhelmed so I can just expose a little of what's really happening with my life.

DAN: Um, usually, you have to [go] down to their [Filipina/os'] social status. You don't talk about money. You also don't let them know like where you live or what kind of car you drive. Sometimes you tell them that, um, when you bought something, it's all on credit, even though you already paid for it. Because people, when they feel as if you're more well to do, um, they treat you differently if you're not like them.

When interacting with Filipina/os, Laura and Dan mentioned they have been cautious in revealing their class identity. Both referred to "downing" or "toning down" their class identity to prevent offending/overwhelming Filipina/os. Dan would not discuss anything related to money—where he lives, the car he owns, etc.—to create an equal footing with his Filipina/o peers. Masking class identity, like in Dan's case, is a form of strategic rhetorical performance. Emerging from "powerful structural positions" (Flores et al., 2006, p. 183), "strategic rhetoric is not itself a place, but it functions to resecure the center" (Nakayama & Krizek, 1995, p. 295). Considering Laura and Dan's comments, both assumed that they could offend Filipina/os if they revealed their class identity. Consequently, they would avoid talking about living in good neighborhoods, driving nice cars, and buying things outright (not on credit) to be perceived positively, which recenters their privileged bodies. Regardless of intent, Laura and Dan's performances do result in a cultural stereotype of Filipina/os as poor, which have "implications on material conditions and arrangements of power" (Flores et al., 2006, p. 183). On the other hand, as Laura and Dan articulated, they often do not want to talk about their class identity to protect themselves from potential backlash if they were to flaunt their privileged lives. I caution, however, that Laura and Dan's experiences do not reflect the lives of all Tsina/oys. Privileged or not, Tsina/oys' class identity is one aspect of their intersectional identities that often leads to experiencing multiple tensions.

(De)Legitimizing Tsina/oy Identity: Negotiating Multiple Tensions

December 2, 2010. After visiting the Chinese Filipina/o museum, Bahay Tsinoy, I have realized that Tsina/oys have faced multiple tensions for generations in the (post)colonial Philippines. From trading to establishing Chinese schools to gaining Filipina/o citizenship, Tsina/oys have managed to embody their hybridity but not without challenges. Being here at Bahay Tsina/oy is a wonderful opportunity for me to talk with Anson who might know about the tensive nature of Tsina/oy identity.

I walk into an office space where Anson welcomes me with great joy. He smiles and asks me if I had visited the museum. I nod my head signaling "yes," and I emphasize how I enjoyed seeing Tsina/oy history and culture come to life. As someone who works with the daily management of Bahay Tsinoy, I can tell Anson's passion for what he does. Anson's friendly personality allows for conversations to happen organically. After learning about my book project on Tsina/oys, Anson reveals to me he was born in Hong Kong, even though his father was from China. Searching for a better economic opportunity, Anson's family immigrated to the Philippines when he was around 14 years old. It took another seven years while finishing college when Anson became a Filipino citizen. While moving in-between transnational spaces, Anson had to find the balance of adapting to a new environment in the Philippines without neglecting his Chinese heritage.

As one can imagine, negotiating both Chinese and Filipina/o identities, especially growing up with immigrant parents, can be challenging for Tsina/oys like Anson. Anson's story is a window to the struggle that many Tsina/oys face for legitimizing their identities as Chinese and Filipina/o. Consequently, multicultural people like Tsina/oys face multiple tensions (Yep, 2002). Multiple tensions could result in Tsina/oys' privileging an aspect of their identity as Chinese or Filipina/o to be accepted by others. In order to understand how Tsina/oys experience multiple tensions, I analyze their hybrid performances based on perceived body markers and the feeling of in-betweenness.

Tsina/oy Bodies: Navigating Ethnic Identities

Privileging Chinese or Filipina/o identity as performance for Tsina/oys can depend on how others read their bodies. Many Tsina/oy participants expressed that it is common for Filipina/os to assume they are Chinese due to their Chinese physical features. In the case of Anthony, he indicated the complexity of performing his hybridity: "But you see, if you were in the Chinese community, you say 'Chinese Filipino.' If I'm in a community of Filipino, they look at my features and they say, 'Yeah, Chinese,' but I tell them 'I'm a Filipino.'" Anthony's experience shows the need to perform and negotiate his Tsinoyness in the company of different ethnic groups. With Chinese individuals, he emphasized the hybrid "Chinese Filipino" to show that his Filipino identity is as much part of his Chinese one. Because there has been a recent surge of Chinese migrants who have established businesses in the Metro Manila area, such as selling goods in 168 and Tutuban shopping malls (See & Chu, 2012), I believe that Anthony must specify "Chinese Filipino" to situate his locality in the Philippines. Distinguishing Tsina/oys from Chinese migrants is what Halualani et al. (2009) would consider as historicizing the locality of ethnic bodies as a sense of belongingness. Given the historical construction of ethnic Chinese in the Philippines as the foreign Other, especially during Spanish and U.S. colonization, it is crucial for some Tsina/oys to make it explicitly known that they are Chinese Filipina/os to communicate their in-group membership.

In the company of Filipina/os, it is not surprising that many Tsina/oys like Anthony would accentuate their Filipino identity to challenge the perceived fixed construction of Chineseness. It is intriguing that Anthony would specifically highlight that he is "Filipino" instead of "Chinese Filipino" while interacting with Filipina/os. I interpret Anthony's performance as a legitimization of his Filipinoness that would otherwise be erased based on his Chinese-looking body. Anthony and other Tsina/oys could be perceived as an out-group should they decide not to identify like other Filipina/os. In fact, Dan also shared his struggles with when and where to call himself "Tsinoy." Even though he would identify as Tsinoy, he revealed to me this concern: "You're still going to say you're Filipino because it's [Tsina/oy] not exactly socially accepted term across all races." In this case, Anthony and Dan would simply say they are "Filipino" among other Filipina/os in order to show they are just like them, which affirms the political nature of hybridity (Anzaldúa, 1999; Pascual, 2004). For Tsina/oys to emphasize their Filipina/o identity in the company of Filipina/os is to privilege an ethnic identity as political performance to be accepted as in-group members.

Tsina/oys can also engage in intercultural performances of their Tsina/oyness. Mike told me how he has identified and negotiated his hybridity:

> I would classify myself "Chinese Filipino," but if someone asked, I would say "Filipino Chinese." Maybe because of, um, they would feel you're more, uh, either you're pure Chinese or more close to Chinese or close to the Filipino. So, they would feel more closer to the Filipino if you impart the word "Filipino."

Identifying as "Chinese Filipino," Mike would reverse the semantic order to "Filipino Chinese" when communicating with others regardless of their ethnicity. His explanation tells me that the rewording could help emphasize a strong affiliation with Filipina/os, even though from a semantic perspective "Filipino Chinese" would have a different meaning from "Chinese Filipino." "Filipino Chinese" would signify a Chinese (noun) of Filipina/o ancestry (modifier), while "Chinese Filipina/o" would describe "Filipinos who are of Chinese cultural descent" (See, 2004, p. 84). Despite Mike's understanding of the differences between the two terms, his use of "Filipino Chinese" is strategic to prioritize his Filipino identity as a public presentation of self to others.

No matter whom they interact with, both Anthony and Mike must perform and negotiate their identities by privileging either their Chinese or Filipino identity so that they can fit in within specific groups of people. As Anthias (2001) attests, hybridity can result in hierarchization to highlight a specific identity in a cultural space. Naturally, privileging Tsina/oys' Chinese identity to call themselves "Chinese Filipino" would be acceptable within the Chinese community, but identifying as "Filipino" or "Filipino Chinese" would be essential if interacting with Filipina/os.

Neither Here Nor There: Feeling In-Between

Because of their hybridity, Tsina/oys often feel like they straddle between Chinese and Filipina/o cultures. Rita and Denisa echoed the tension they have felt for being "half-half" and "in-between," respectively. Like other Tsina/oys, Laura has struggled with her cultural hybridity:

> Well, I just feel that it's hard to be a, um, from Chinese descendant born in the Philippines because I really don't belong to the Chinese [laughs], um, community, but

> I also don't belong to the Filipino community. I cannot totally embrace the Filipino community also, so when I was young, like when I was small, I feel lost, like, I'm just questioning, "Most people they are Filipinos born in the Philippines. Why am I Chinese born in the Philippines?" I'm so confused, yeah, so but right now I feel that, um, it's how you look at it. It's also a blessing like I adopt whatever...whatever is, um, the good points with being a Filipino or Chinese, I adopt all these things. Anyway, everybody is the same, right? So...[laughs]. So, I just feel that, um, we just have to think of it in a positive way.

It is difficult for Laura to constantly shift her body to fit into Chinese and Filipina/o communities. Many Tsina/oys experience the volleying effect of negotiating "multiple roles and identities" (Alexander, 2002, p. 19). As a Filipina citizen, she has struggled to be accepted as Chinese, and her Chinese-looking body has made it difficult for her to legitimize her Filipina identity. Laura's experience resonates with how I negotiate my Tsinoy identity in different cultural contexts. While living in the Philippines, my Chinese-appearing body prevented some Filipina/os to see me as one of them, even though I am Filipino and speak Tagalog (Hao, 2021). While visiting China as a tourist, my body blended in, but my inability to speak Mandarin fluently resulted in me being read as Other. In these cultural moments of interaction, I contend the "issue of authenticity is not about what is real as much as what is known" (Alexander, 2006, p. 19). The similarity of experiences between Laura and me proves that our bodies operate as texts that can be read in specific ways that correspond to in-group members' cultural expectations.

Multiple tensions can also be attributed to Tsina/oys' performance of Chinese and Filipina/o cultural practices. "I'm Chinese, but verbally I'm more Filipino. It depends on where I am and what I do," said Martha. Like many Tsina/oys, Martha has grappled with her hybrid identity in which her Chineseness can be attributed to her body, cultural values, and/or traditions. On the other hand, her fluency in Tagalog as opposed to Mandarin has made her feel more Filipina in that respect. Martha's experience is not unusual with younger Tsina/oys, many of whom do not want to learn Mandarin and cannot speak Hokkien. In fact, "The younger generation [of Tsina/oys] starts picking up the ability [to speak Hokkien], though with some difficulty, only when they start entering the business world, especially if they become involved in trading activities" (See, 1997b, p. 94).

It is also worth noting that transnationalism can also contribute to Tsina/oys' multiple tensions. Carol gave a snapshot of what it was like as a Tsinay living in a different country that affected her performance of hybridity:

> Sometimes, I feel I'm more Chinese in certain situations. Then sometimes I feel more Filipino...But now after three years there [in Japan and] coming back [to the Philippines], I can really say I feel more Chinese than Filipino. Now that I'm back, I started...I started to feel like again I'm more Chinese than Filipino, which is weird. When I was outside the Philippines, I feel sometimes more Filipino, sometimes more Chinese. Because I'm back here, I feel more Chinese than Filipino. I'm with the family, and with the family, we all speak Chinese...maybe that.

Carol's experience demonstrates how a family's influence and living in a different country can have a significant impact on one's hybridity. Surrounded by Tsina/oy family members who speak Hokkien at home, Carol stated she feels more Chinese than Filipina in the Philippines. However, Carol was able to perform her Chinese and Filipina identities with some flexibility in Japan. First, due to the lack of her family's presence, she did not have to embody her Chineseness the same way as she would in the Philippines. Second, I believe performing hybridity in unfamiliar places can be liberating because one does not have to embody specific cultural performances in the presence of in-group members. In instances like Carol's, hybridity "retains a sense of difference and tension between two cultures but without assuming hierarchy. It is not just a new identity but a new form of identity" (Sakamoto, 1996, pp. 115–116). Keeping Sakamoto's (1996) words in mind, Carol was able to perform "a new form of identity" (p. 116) where both Chinese and Filipina identities emerged more fluidly in Japan than in the Philippines. By contrast, upon returning to the Philippines, she had to readjust by performing Chinese identity that would conform to her family's expected behaviors. Carol's story exemplifies a new form of Tsina/oy identity that connects the past and present based on its embodiment in (trans)national spaces (Bhabha, 1997).

Returning Home

December 16, 2010. The phone rings in the living room, and my grandmother informs me that a driver is waiting downstairs to take me to the airport. I take a moment to check the guest room that became my home for the last couple of weeks to make sure I have not left anything behind. My grandmother reminds me to secure my passport and other documents. Assuring her I have everything in place, I hug and thank my grandmother for making me feel at home.

While riding the van to the airport, I reflect on my stay in Manila. Returning to the country of my birth brought back so many childhood memories, but more importantly being here reminded me of who I am. I also learned a great deal interacting with other Tsina/oys for understanding different perspectives on what it means to be (trans)national hybrids. Keeping the Critical Intercultural Performance (CIP) framework in mind, I emphasized the intersectionality of ethnic, national, and class identities to analyze diverse Tsina/oy experiences. However, I acknowledge that addressing gender as a part of the intersectional Tsina/oy identity warrants more attention than what I have provided in my analysis. An extensive discussion of gender identity would have provided another perspective to the complexity of Tsina/oyness as it is performed across ethnic and (trans)national lines.

As another commitment to CIP, I practiced reflexivity by considering my privileged background as a U.S. educated Tsinoy when interpreting Tsina/oy voices. My ethnographic interviews with Tsina/oys provided me insights to what "Tsina/oy" means culturally, socially, and politically. Most participants were receptive to the term "Tsina/oy"; however, a few challenged its potential limitations to keep up with current and future evolution of Tsina/oy identity. Tsina/oy participants also discussed how they have experienced multiple tensions due to their hybridity's negotiated performances between social identities and self (Hall, 1994). More specifically, some of the tensions have resulted in privileging one identity over another. They also shared the feeling of isolation for not being able to fit into respective Chinese and Filipina/o communities. However, many Tsina/oy participants have coped with negotiating their identities by celebrating the positive aspects of hybridity.

One positive aspect of my hybrid body is its ability to move across (trans)national spaces and homes. It took me 17 years to come back to Manila, so leaving again is bittersweet. Upon arriving at Ninoy Aquino International Airport, I exit the van and go into the airport terminal to check in my luggage and get my boarding passes. With layover flights in Tokyo and Los Angeles before arriving in Denver, I am reminded of my (trans)national body who will be returning to another home. After spending a couple of weeks in Manila, I feel my body is transitioning back to a different, but familiar, cultural space. Perhaps this is what it means to be a (trans)national Tsinoy whose (e)merging Chinese and Filipino identities prompt me to recognize the fluid but contradictory nature of my multicultural self.

References

Alexander, B. K. (2002). Betwixt & between: The liminal space of the graduate student as administrative assistant. In W. Davis, J. Smith, & R. Smith (Eds.), *Ready to teach: Gaduate teaching assistants prepare for today and for tomorrow* (pp. 16–20). New Forums Press.

Alexander, B. K. (2006). *Performing black masculinity: Race, culture, and queer identity.* AltaMira Press.

Anthias, F. (2001). New hybridities, old concepts: The limits of "culture." *Ethnic and Racial Studies, 24*(4), 619–641. https://doi.org/10.1080/01419870120049815

Anzaldúa, G. (1999). *Borderlands/La frontera: The new mestiza* (2nd ed.). Aunt Lute Books.

Bakhtin, M. M. (1981). *The dialogic imagination: Four essays* (C. Emerson & M. Holquist, Trans.). University of Texas Press.

Bautista, R., & Lema, K. (2018, January 28). Philippines to phase out its beloved cheap but rickety jeepneys. *Reuters.* https://www.reuters.com/article/us-philippines-transport-jeepneys-idUSKBN1FI0IJ

Bernal, M. E., & Knight, G. (Eds.). (1993). *Ethnic identity.* State University of New York Press.

Bhabha, H. (1994). *The location of culture.* Routledge.

Bhabha, H. (1997). Life at the border: Hybrid identities of the present. *New Perspectives Quarterly, 14*(1), 30–31.

Butler, J. (1988). Performative acts and gender constitution: An essay in phenomenology and feminist theory. *Theory Journal, 40*(4), 519–531. https://doi.org/10.2307/3207893

Butler, J. (1990). Performative acts and gender constitution: An essay in phenomenology and feminist theory. In S. E. Case (Ed.), *Performing feminisms: Feminist critical theory and theatre* (pp. 270–282). Johns Hopkins University Press.

Calafell, B. M. (2004). Disrupting the dichotomy: 'Yo soy Chicana/o?' in the new Latina/o south. *Communication Review, 7*(2), 175–204. https://doi.org/10.1080/10714420490448705

Cariño, T. C. (2001). The Philippines. In E. T. Gomez & H.-H. M. Hsiao (Ed.), *Chinese business in Southeast Asia: Contesting cultural explanations, researching entrepreneurship* (pp. 101–123). Curzon.

Chua, A. (2003). *World on fire: How exporting free market democracy breeds ethnic hatred and global instability.* First Anchor Books.

Cupach, W. R., & Imahori, T. T. (1993). Identity management theory: Communication competence in intercultural episodes and relationships. In R. L. Wiseman & J. Koester (Eds.), *Intercultural communication competence* (pp. 112–131). SAGE.

Flores, L. A., Moon, D. G., & Nakayama, T. K. (2006). Dynamic rhetorics of race: California's Racial Privacy Initiative and the shifting grounds of racial politics. *Communication and Critical/Cultural Studies, 3*(3), 181–201. https://doi.org/10.1080/14791420600841351

Gordon, N. S. (2016). Reggae 3.0: Social media and the consumption of Jamaican popular culture. In K. Sorrells & S. Sekimoto (Eds.), *Globalizing intercultural communication: A reader* (pp. 228–238). SAGE.

Guillermo, A. R. (2012). *Historical dictionary of the Philippines* (3rd ed.). Scarecrow Press.

Hall, S. (1990). Cultural identity and diaspora. In J. Rutherford (Ed.), *Identity: Community, culture, difference* (pp. 222–237). Lawrence and Wishart.

Hall, S. (1994). Cultural identity and diasporas. In P. Williams & L. Chrisman (Eds.), *Colonial discourse and postcolonial theory* (pp. 394–402). Columbia University Press.

Halualani, R. T. (2008) "Where exactly is the Pacific?": Global migrations, diasporic movements, and intercultural communication. *Journal of International and Intercultural Communication, 1*(1), 3–22. https://doi.org/10.1080/17513050701739509

Halualani, R. T., Mendoza, S. L., & Drzewiecka, J. A. (2009). "Critical" junctures in intercultural communication studies: A review. *The Review of Communication, 9*(1), 17–35. https://doi.org/10.1080/15358590802169504

Hao, R. N. (2020). Critical intercultural performance framework: Transnational hybridity as performance of reentries. *Journal of Intercultural Communication Research, 49*(5), 425–432. https://doi.org/10.1080/17475759.2020.1798804

Hao, R. N. (2021). Performing fortune cookie: An autoethnographic performance on diasporic hybridity. In R. M. Boylorn & M. P. Orbe (Eds.), *Critical autoethnography: Intersecting cultural identities in everyday life* (2nd ed., pp. 45–56). Routledge.

hooks, b. (1990). *Yearning: Race, gender, and cultural politics*. South End Press.

Kraidy, M. M. (2005). *Hybridity, or the cultural logic of globalization*. Temple University Press.

Lan, P. (2003). Maid or madam?: Filipina migrant workers and the continuity of domestic labor. *Gender & Society, 17*(2), 187–208. https://doi.org/10.1177/0891243202250730

Madison, D. S., & Hamera, J. (2006). Performance studies at the intersections. In D. S. Madison & J. Hamera (Eds.), *The SAGE handbook of performance studies* (pp. xi–xxv). SAGE.

Martin, J. N., & Nakayama, T. K. (2018). *Experiencing intercultural communication: An introduction* (6th ed.). McGraw-Hill Education.

Mendoza, S. L., Halualani, R. T., & Drzewiecka, J. A. (2002). Moving the discourse on identities in intercultural communication: Structure, culture, and resignifications. *Communication Quarterly, 50*(3–4), 312–327. https://doi.org/10.1080/01463370209385666

Nakayama, T. K., & Krizek, R. L. (1995). Whiteness: A strategic rhetoric. *Quarterly Journal of Speech, 81*(3), 291–309. https://doi.org/10.1080/00335639509384117

Nam, V. (2001). *Yell-oh girls!: Emerging voices explore culture, identity, and growing up Asian American*. HarperCollins.

Parreñas, R. S. (2000). Migrant Filipina domestic workers and the international division of reproductive labor. *Gender & Society, 14*(4), 560–580. https://doi.org/10.1177/089124300014004005

Pascual, M. R. (2004). Traversing disparate cultures in a transnational world. In A. González, M. Houston, & V. Chen (Eds.), *Our voices: Essays on culture, ethnicity, and communication* (4th ed., pp. 288–297). Roxbury.

Sakamoto, R. (1996). Japan, hybridity, and the creation of colonialist discourse. *Theory, Culture, and Society, 13*(3), 113–128. https://doi.org/10.1177/026327696013003006

See, T. A. (1997a). *Chinese in the Philippines: Problems & perspectives* (Vol. 1). Kaisa Para Sa Kaunlaran.

See, T. A. (1997b). *Chinese in the Philippines: Problems & perspectives* (Vol. 2). Kaisa Para Sa Kaunlaran.

See, T. A. (2004). *Chinese in the Philippines: Problems & perspectives* (Vol. 3). Kaisa Para Sa Kaunlaran.

See, T. A., & Chu, R. T. (2012). An overview of Binondo's history. *Manila, 8*(1). Retrieved from https://ejournals.ph/article.php?id=3175

Shi, Y. (2005). Identity construction of the Chinese diaspora, ethnic media use, community formation, and the possibility of social activism. *Continuum: Journal of Media & Cultural Studies, 19*(1), 55–72. https://doi.org/10.1080/1030431052000336298

Shome, R., & Hegde, R. (2002). Culture, communication, and the challenge of globalization. *Critical Studies in Media Communication, 19*(2), 172–189. https://doi.org/10.1080/07393180216560

Tan, A. S. (1988). The changing identity of the Philippine Chinese, 1946–1984. In J. Cushman & G. Wang (Eds.), *Changing identities of the Southeast Asian Chinese since World War II* (pp. 177–203). Hong Kong University Press.

Tankei-Aminian, S. (2016). On becoming *Japersican*: A personal narrative of cultural adaptation, intercultural identity, and transnationalism. In K. Sorrells & S. Sekimoto (Eds.), *Globalizing intercultural communication: A reader* (pp. 197–205). SAGE.

Uytanlet, J. L. (2016). *The hybrid Tsinoys: Challenges of hybridity and homogeneity as sociocultural constructs among the Chinese in the Philippines*. Pickwick.

Yap, J. P. (2018). The troubled dual construction of ethnicity of recent Chinese migrants and third generation Chinese-Filipinos in Binondo, Manila. *Mabini Review, 7*, 166–198.

Yep, G. A. (2002). My three cultures: Navigating the multicultural identity landscape. In J. N. Martin, T. K. Nakayama, & L. A. Flores (Eds.), *Readings in intercultural communication: Experiences and contexts* (2nd ed., pp. 60–66). McGraw-Hill.

Yep, G. A. (2016). Toward thick(er) intersectionalities: Theorizing, researching, and activating the complexities of communication and identities. In K. Sorrells & S. Sekimoto (Eds.), *Globalizing intercultural communication: A reader* (pp. 86–94). SAGE.

Young, S. L. (2009). Half and half: An (auto)ethnography of hybrid identities in a Korean American mother-daughter relationship. *Journal of International and Intercultural Communication, 2*(2), 139–167. https://doi.org/10.1080/17513050902759512

BECOMING TSINOY AMERICAN: (TRANS)NATIONAL IDENTITY AND CITIZENSHIP

July 20, 2016. I march along following the "To the Lobby" sign at the Los Angeles Convention Center. As I continue to walk in a 90-degree-Fahrenheit weather, I see another sign directing me to the "Citizenship" area. Finally getting to my destination, I can hear the U.S. Citizenship and Immigration Services (USCIS) officials directing applicants and their families to walk on left and right sides, respectively. I continue to walk as instructed that leads me to a big arena that resembles an airport security screening area. Stepping into the farthest left lane, I place all my personal items inside of a light gray rectangular bin for screening. Getting the clearance, I proceed to my right and enter a double door that takes me to another room. I immediately see tables on my left lined up one after another with USCIS officers sitting behind them. An officer informs me and others to go all the way to the end. I stop at a table numbered 21, and an officer calls me momentarily to step closer to him. Like a scripted speech that he must have said many times before, the officer asks me to present him my appointment notice and permanent residency card. He then encircles the important details of the notice—my address and appointment date and time—with a blue crayon. He reviews the back page of my notice to ensure I have responded to the questionnaire.

With the appointment notice verified, the USCIS officer inspects my permanent residency card to make sure the picture matches me. He punches a hole in my permanent residency card, making it invalid. He then stamps my appointment notice with the following instruction: "After the Oath Ceremony please proceed to the table number above." Along with the same stamp, I see "109" written on my appointment notice to let me know where to pick up my Naturalization Certificate later.

I proceed to walk with other attendees who are going through the motion as other USCIS officials directing us where to sit. "All the way down! All the way down!" chants one official ordering us not to skip any seat. I sit in a chair from the left edge of the row. Everyone sits so tightly next to one another that I can barely move. Despite the packed room, I am delighted to see diverse attendees who come from all over the world and different age groups. Many are dressed professionally like they are going to a job interview, while others have opted for a casual attire. Like me, attendees in the room appear to be smiling and enjoying the special moment. While sitting still, I can't help but notice a big projected screen in front of us showing an image of the U.S. flag with the message: "Celebrate Citizenship, Celebrate America." Today's occasion marks a milestone for everyone attending the Oath of Allegiance ceremony to celebrate what it means to become a U.S. American.

Even though I have lived in the United States for more than two decades, I did not think about becoming a U.S. citizen as soon as I was eligible to do so in 2012. However, when Donald Trump ran for the U.S. presidency, my sense of urgency changed when he proposed banning Muslims from entering the United States (Barro, 2015) and building a "wall" along the U.S.-Mexico border (Allen, 2016). Trump's anti-immigration rhetoric made me think about my own immigration status, even as a permanent resident of the United States. As a non-U.S. citizen, a part of me was thinking about the possibility of being separated from my spouse and son. In fact, the rhetoric of immigrant deportability has historically communicated that "bodies are racialized" and goes beyond "legal parameters, circulating discursively, fixing bodies (often regardless of residency status) within it" (Flores & Gomez, 2020, p. 202). While I do not claim that my immigration status was comparable to that of other immigrants, I agree with Flores and Gomez that the rhetoric of deportability, especially in the age of Trump, often politicized immigrants of color as a threat to "real" U.S. Americans (p. 201). My fear for the possibility of family separation resulted in my personal decision to apply for U.S. citizenship in 2016. Although going through the legal process of becoming a U.S. citizen was not challenging for me, I experienced cultural tensions for simultaneously losing and gaining a national identity. Writing from critical autoethnographic accounts, I analyze how my participation in the Oath of Allegiance ceremony, more specifically, has affected my conceptualization of the Tsinoy body, (trans)national hybridity, and citizenship. To start, I provide a brief historical overview and personal description of the Oath of Allegiance ceremony. Reflecting from the Oath of Allegiance ceremony, I delve into what it means to be a *balikbayan* or cultural returnee to help me understand my (trans)national hybridity. I end the chapter by examining how the Oath of Allegiance ceremony has impacted my understanding of Tsinoy American identity.

Oath of Allegiance: A Performance of U.S. Citizenship

Since the first naturalization law was enacted in 1790, foreigners "have taken an oath to support the Constitution of the United States" (U.S. Citizenship and Immigration Services [USCIS], 2020, para. 2). The Naturalization Act of 1795 followed requiring "an applicant to declare an intention (commitment) to become U.S. citizen before filing a Petition for Naturalization," which would require taking an Oath of Allegiance to the United States to "renounce (give up) any allegiance to foreign prince, potentate, state, or sovereignty. Applicants born with a hereditary title also had to renounce their title or order of nobility" (para. 2). Because there was no uniformity among the courts performing the oath, each court could develop its own procedures and only had to certify that applicants took an oath.

The Basic Naturalization Act of 1906 included the new Declaration of Intention and Petition for Naturalization forms to emphasize "some of the substance of the oath" in which applicants recited the oath (USCIS, 2020, para. 6). In addition, the Basic Naturalization Act required "new citizens to defend the Constitution and laws of the United States of America against all enemies, foreign and domestic; and bear true faith and allegiance to the same" (para. 6). In 1929 the official text for the Oath of Allegiance became a requirement for applicants to recite in court before they could receive their naturalization certificate. The Immigration Act of 1950 added language about "bearing arms on behalf of the United States when required by the law; and performing noncombatant service in the armed forces of the United States when required by the law" (para. 9). However, based on religious training and beliefs, applicants who oppose bearing arms or performing noncombatant service can request an exemption "from taking the full oath of allegiance" (para. 9). The last addition to the oath, which is "about performing work of national importance under civilian direction," was instituted as a result of the Immigration and Nationality Act of 1952 (para. 10).

With my understanding of the Oath of Allegiance, I wait patiently for the ceremony to start. I sit still with 4,000 other participants from 134 countries. A few minutes past one o'clock in the afternoon, an African American man in a black suit walks to the podium greeting everyone "Good Afternoon." He proceeds with the announcement that the ceremony will happen momentarily as soon as the judge arrives. The waiting period has been filled with the projection of a video recording and still images. The video showcases recent naturalized citizens smiling and waving small U.S. flags. A Honduran American sergeant remarks in the video with pride: "My fellow soldiers made me feel I was an American. I definitely stand proud and army strong as ever." A Canadian naturalized U.S. citizen adds, "America has provided me a special opportunity with the freedom to choose my path." The video concludes how it began: naturalized U.S. citizens are featured once again waving U.S. flags. The video depicts a whiteness performance of U.S. citizenship, which McIntosh et al. (2020) refer to as the universal construction of "American Dream" that can be attained by everyone. Although I feel uncomfortable watching the staged production of what it means to gain a U.S. citizenship, wherever I turn, other participants show enthusiasm and pride while attending the oath ceremony.

The same African American man who appeared on stage earlier walks back to the podium, and this time he introduces the judge, a White American man wearing a traditional black robe, who is presiding to conduct the Oath of Allegiance. The judge instructs attendees to stand up and raise our right hand. He recites the oath word for word:

> I hereby declare, on oath, that I absolutely and entirely renounce and abjure all allegiance and fidelity to any foreign prince, potentate, State, or sovereignty of whom or which I have heretofore been a subject or citizen; that I will support and defend the Constitution and laws of the United States of America against all enemies, foreign and domestic; that I will bear true faith and allegiance to the same; that I will bear arms on behalf of the United States when required by the law; that I will perform noncombatant service in the Armed Forces of the United States when required by the law; that I will perform work of national importance under civilian direction when required by the law; and that I take this obligation freely without any mental reservation or purpose of evasion: So help me God. Congratulations!

Everyone applauds with great enthusiasm. While I clap to join other participants' excitement for completing the oath ceremony, I remain uneasy. With my multicultural identities, I feel "tensions across points of cultural difference" (Durham, 2004, p. 141) for being asked to show my loyalty to one nation, which delegitimizes my Filipino identity. With other Filipina/o Americans about to become naturalized citizens today, I wonder if they feel the same tension since many of us consider ourselves (trans)national hybrids whose bodies are constantly in movement between two homes.

The judge asks us to be seated. Unlike the rest of us sitting before him, the U.S.-born judge notes that he has been privileged all his life for not having to go through "the hard way" of becoming a U.S. citizen. He talks about how he is not as "American" as those of us who have worked hard and waited so long to do the interview, demonstrated good character, and been tested on our system of government. Aware of the growing anti-immigrant rhetoric plaguing the United States a few months before the 2016 presidential election, the judge ends with a solemn note of the unfortunate times we currently live in where many people are fearful of immigrants.

Performing *Balikbayan* Identity: (Trans)national Tsina/oys as Cultural Returnees

Hearing the judge's words reminds me of the long journey I have taken to become a naturalized citizen of the United States. As an immigrant who has acquired a new national identity, it does not change that my body is still (trans)national in nature, especially as someone who travels between the Philippines and the United States. Because I consider both the Philippines and the United States as homes, it is important for me to also examine my (trans)national Tsinoy identity as a *balikbayan* or cultural returnee.

Six years earlier on December 8, 2010, I met one of my cousins for dinner while staying in Manila. The last time I saw him was when we were both teenagers, so I was excited to reunite with him. I texted him the address to my grandmother and aunt's apartment. A few minutes past 6 o'clock at night, my cousin informed me that he will be arriving shortly. Exiting the apartment building, I spotted him after rolling down his car's passenger window. He smiled and greeted me enthusiastically, "Long time no see!" I responded, "*Oo nga*" ["Yes, indeed"]. Impressed that I could still speak Tagalog, he asked if I had any food preference. As someone who can eat different cuisines, I told my cousin in English: "I'm okay with anything." He decided to take me to a Filipina/o restaurant in the business district of Makati. Taking almost an hour to get there during rush hour traffic, we arrived at a modern Filipina/o restaurant. The ambience was a fusion of traditional and modern furnishings and decor that reflected the postcolonial Philippines. After being seated, a waiter handed each of us a menu. The waiter asked us if we needed some time to look through the menu. My cousin interjected immediately, "*Ano ang pagrerekomenda mo para sa balikbayan?*" ["What would you recommend to a returnee?"].

Upon hearing my cousin's remark, I was caught off guard. It was not until I met with my cousin that I became aware of my identity as a *balikbayan*, or a (trans)national returnee from the United States. *Balikbayan* is derived from "*balik*," which means "to return" in Tagalog and "*bayan*" refers to the "Philippine nation" (Blanc, 1996, p. 178). Combining "*balik*" and "*bayan*" together, *balikbayans* are "'returnees,' people coming back home to the Philippines" (p. 178). However, *balikbayans* can also refer to "Filipino[s] visiting or returning to the Philippines after a period of living in another country" (English Oxford Living Dictionaries, 2016).

Historically, *balikbayan* as a cultural returnee identity was also developed to foster economic ties between Filipina/os abroad and locally. In fact, former President Ferdinand Marcos created the *Balikbayan* Program in the Philippines

> to attract Filipino-American tourists back to the Philippines. It has since become the most important source of foreign exchange, skills and income for the Philippines. The program, supported by subsequent presidents, has progressively united under similar regulations overseas contract workers (OCWs) such as nurses and technicians going to the United States, construction and service workers going to the Middle East, etc., and long-term migrants of Philippine background who have settled or were born in the United States, Canada, Europe, Australia, and other foreign countries and have by now often become foreign nationals. (Blanc, 1996, p. 178)

In addition to its cultural and economic conceptualizations, the meaning of *balikbayan* has evolved over the years. In 1980 only Filipina/os, their families, and children who are citizens and permanent residents of other countries were considered *balikbayans* (Blanc, 1996). The definition of *balikbayan* was revised again in 1989, which has remained the same since then:

> 1) A Filipino citizen who has been continuously out of the Philippines for a period of at least one year from date of last departure; 2) a Filipino overseas worker; or 3) a

former Filipino citizen and his family (spouse and children), who had been naturalized in a foreign country and who visit or return to the Philippines. (p. 181)

Balikbayans are (trans)national hybrids that communicate "the concept of nation well beyond its territorial boundaries" to build connections between different cultural homes (p. 183). As a result of the historical immigration patterns of Filipina/os in the United States and other countries, it is not unusual for *balikbayans* to have families in the current country of residence and Philippines. In-between cultural spaces provide *balikbayans* opportunities to establish personal and professional communities (trans)nationally. To this end, thinking of Anderson's (1983) work, *balikbayans* are defining Filipina/o national identity beyond the Philippines as a nation-state by reconstituting their belongingness to various cultural spaces.

Given that *balikbayans* are (trans)national hybrids who travel between cultural homes, it is appropriate to examine literature on cultural reentry. Cultural reentry has been defined as the return or transition of sojourners to their home culture (Gama & Pedersen, 1977; Martin, 1984). Because not all returnees, such as *balikbayans*, return home permanently, Chang (2010) points out that a gap in cultural reentry literature exists because of "its exclusive focus on permanent returns, disregarding temporary reentries. As a result, we have little knowledge of short-term reentry experiences, which are becoming increasingly frequent" (p. 169). That said, how does cultural reentry impact the way we conceptualize "home culture"? What if one has multiple homes? If a *balikbayan* is only in the Philippines for one week or a few weeks, does that experience count as cultural reentry? As a *balikbayan* who has visited the Philippines for a short period of time, these questions motivate me to examine what's lacking in the current literature of cultural reentry and offer possibilities in understanding the complexity of (trans)national bodies in transit.

The predominant theme in the current literature on cultural reentry is that of host/home binary (Hao, 2012), which is exemplified in studies that focus on the experiences of U.S. students returning home from host countries (Martin, 1986; Rohrlich & Martin, 1991; Smith, 2001; Tomlin et al., 2014; Wilson, 1993), non-U.S. international students who go back home after their schooling experiences (Brabant et al., 1990; Chang, 2010; Rogers & Ward, 1993), and business executives returning home after working abroad (Adler, 1981; Black et al., 1992; Harvey, 1989). For instance, Martin's (1986) study "examined 173 student sojourners' perceptions of their communication in three types of reentry relationships (with parents, siblings, and friends)" (p. 183). The student sojourners were surveyed to "(1) evaluate their current communication and (2) describe specific communication changes in these relationships" (p. 183). Martin's study focused on using the role of communication because most of the literature on cultural reentry primarily examined it from a socio-psychological process when individuals adapt to the home culture. While Martin acknowledged the "fluidity and ever-changing nature of human relationships" (p. 184), her work in cultural reentry drew primarily from relational communication literature that emphasizes that there are "stages" that returnees experience to accomplish successful cultural transition.

Contrary to Martin's study, Kim's (2000, 2002) theory of cross-cultural adaptation considers adaptation as cyclical rather than linear in which returnees experience multiple feelings and behaviors; as a result, they are essentially transformed interculturally in the process. Kim's theory of cross-cultural adaptation has become influential in reentry studies because it emphasizes the notion that adaptation is complex and should be understood contextually, but the main drawback with Kim's theory and other studies on cultural reentry is that they tend to discuss sojourners who return to their home permanently, which reinforces that there is one and only home that one returns to. My critique of Kim's cross-cultural adaptation reminds of Clifford's (1992) problematization of the need to distinguish local from global:

> Some strategy of localization is inevitable if significantly different ways of life are to be represented. But "local" in whose terms? How is significant difference politically articulated, and challenged? Who determines where (and when) a community draws its lines, names its insiders and outsiders? (p. 97)

Perhaps that is why Chang (2010) reinforces that it is important to examine short-term reentry because "the duration of stay may influence returnees' motivation to readapt to their home culture, which may affect their interaction with others and, hence, their reentry experiences" (p. 169). To fill these gaps, Chang's study "explores the experiences of mothers of study abroad students in China interacting with their returnee children during their short-term reentries" (pp. 169–170). As part of the analysis, Chang cites Simmel's (1950) work on strangers in which Chinese mothers saw their returnee children as strangers because they are "physically close but psychologically different" based on their perceived changed values and behaviors (p. 172). Like Chang (2010), Eguchi and Baig (2018) stress that short-term reentries do occur, as I experienced when I visited the Philippines. Even though I came back to the place where I was born and raised, I did not return there permanently.

Current literature on cultural reentry tends to frame reentry as permanent and home as the sole destination to which one ultimately returns (Hao, 2012). In my own personal example, I have multiple homes: Manila, Philippines (birthplace) and Los Angeles, California, United States (current place of residence). It is hard for me to categorize Los Angeles simply as host culture and Manila as home culture. As Clifford (1992) reminds us, "Everyone [is] more or less permanently in transit...Not so much 'where are you from?' but 'where are you between?' (The intercultural identity question)" (p. 109). Clifford's point suggests that we enter in and out of a place or cross borders to create a space where multiple identities are negotiated. I travel in between spaces that allow me to be (re)connected to my birthplace and current place of residence. Although I currently do not live in the Philippines, it is still my homeplace (hooks, 1994) because I have extended family members there that makes it feasible for me to become (re)acquainted with my childhood memories and cultural traditions. According to Kinefuchi (2010), home can be understood as "physically or territorially marked" and symbolically that has "emotional, relational, cultural, and political significances" (p. 231). When I made a trip to Manila in 2010 for the first time since my family and I immigrated to the United States, I knew I was home as soon as I had arrived. Upon exiting Ninoy Aquino International Airport, I heard the familiar noise of crowded streets filled with cars, jeepneys, buses, and taxis; all of which are emotional symbols of why I consider Manila as home. When I got to my grandmother's apartment, located in Manila's Chinatown neighborhood of Binondo, it quickly reminded me of home and my Chinese identity while communicating with my Chinese grandmother in her native tongue. Reuniting with relatives whom I had not seen since I was a child also created a sense of belonging to what it means to be home. The sights and experiences I had encountered confirm that Manila is still home two decades later as if I was traveling in time when I was still a child. Perhaps Kinefuchi (2010) could not have said it better: "Home, in short, consists of emotional, relational, sociocultural, and political spheres, and it is through the working of these spheres that identity is formed" (p. 231).

Even though we can recognize that short-term reentry does occur, the fact remains that there is still the dichotomous relationship between home and host cultures (Hao, 2012). As a result, multicultural individuals experience the categorization of "strangers" when they come "home." For instance, my cousin's labeling of my identity as a *balikbayan* defined me as someone who no longer lives in the Philippines permanently. Without embodying a localized Tsinoy identity, my body could be marked as a "stranger" in the eyes of others. This begs the question of who is the stranger and in what ways? Is one's stranger status based on the fixed notion of where "home" is? According to Berry's (1999) assimilation strategy in acculturation, one's changed values can be performed in different ways, such as altering one's physical appearance and changing norms or rules in social interactions. An example Chang (2010) gives is that Chinese student returnees' "personal style of communicating with their mothers was not satisfactory to the mothers [,]" even though the student returnees "had learned basic social courtesy for interacting with others in society" (p. 174). Chang's study makes me think about how I had to negotiate my Tsinoy and U.S. American identities when interacting with Chinese Filipina/os in the Philippines. While I grew up learning some of the basic mannerisms, my "cultural slippage" was evident when I handed out my business card to a Tsinoy participant with one hand. As soon as I did that, my aunt called me out for being impolite while joking that I had forgotten my cultural manners while being away in the United States for so long. In that moment, no matter how much I had to negotiate (or code switch) my body, I slipped through the cracks as someone who was different. However, I didn't see myself as a stranger in the Philippines. I was able to communicate in local languages with different people who commended me for not losing myself (perhaps during the acculturation process in the United States). In fact, some of my participants and relatives thought that I sounded more Chinese than their children because they didn't seem to want to learn Hokkien. I was surprised to find out that I fit right into the Tsina/oy culture for being able to speak Hokkien and Tagalog effectively among my participants and other people I interacted with, which demonstrated my connection to home and Tsina/oy community. Despite experiencing cultural slippage, I was not a stranger as a returnee to the place where I used to live as a child.

Upon reflecting on the moment of being able to claim myself as a member of the in-group, I started wondering about my parents' efforts to make sure that my siblings and I retained our Tsina/oy culture. Although my siblings and I spent our childhood in Manila, my parents continued to instill the significance of understanding both Chinese and Filipina/o cultures while living in Los Angeles. As an example, speaking in Hokkien and Tagalog at home during my teenage years helped preserve my Tsina/oyness. Is that one of the reasons why I can still speak my native tongues well enough to "pass" as one of the Tsina/oys? I suppose my own upbringing in Los Angeles allowed me to perform my Tsinoyness, especially at home.

On the other hand, technological changes and globalization continue to influence Tsina/oys in the Philippines to become more "U.S. Americans" by following "U.S. American" ways of being (Hao, 2012). I theorize that one way for Tsina/oys to become more "U.S. Americans" is to speak more English than local languages. So, in the Philippines, I was not the strange one, but those who no longer could speak Hokkien in the way I could while I was brought up in the Philippines and the United States. In essence, they were not the Tsina/oys I remember growing up. Yet, at the same time, I think they were becoming like me in terms of speaking more English than our native tongues, which could also explain why I was not a stranger to Tsina/oys in the Philippines.

When I returned to the United States, I started "slipping" into my Tagalog and Hokkien tongues when speaking to people who didn't speak these languages, which illustrated my body's in-betweenness. Having lived a part of my life in the Philippines and the United States, I consider both as my homes. Even though each has different meanings to me culturally and personally, both the Philippines and the United States have shaped my (trans)national hybridity. Halualani (2008) reminds us: "If…migration is conceptualized by many groups as a distinctive cultural act, we should now explore how 'culture' and 'cultural identity' have incorporated globalized change and become a shifting dynamic field that refuses geographic specificity yet remembers a cultural past" (p. 19). Halualani's words emphasize what I think of the (trans)national nature of returnees' cultural identities, which makes it inevitable for returnees to belong to multiple cultural spaces that bridge their past and present selves. No matter where I am, I find my hybrid body to be home in the Philippines and the United States due to familial and cultural connections.

Gaining and Losing a National Identity

July 20, 2016. It has been almost six years since my first trip to the Philippines. Today marks another important juncture in my life as a (trans)national hybrid. As much as it is a joyous occasion to become a U.S. citizen, I feel some tension when reciting the Oath of Allegiance, which communicates one's identification with and loyalty to the United States as a nation-state. As I stand raising my right hand, I hear the judge's same exact words from my application for naturalization five months ago. It should be routine of simply repeating the words I had read, agreed, and signed, but, for whatever reason, I feel uneasiness as soon as I hear the part about renouncing my allegiance to any "foreign…state, or sovereignty of whom or which I have heretofore been a subject or citizen." An initial thought comes to mind: The Philippines is not simply any "foreign" state to me. I was born and raised there; it is my home. Hall (1996) articulates how individuals experience "new ethnicities" in transnational spaces that question and challenge what "nation" means to them. After all, "'home' is inseparable from immigrant identity formation" (Kinefuchi, 2010, p. 230), which reminds me of my (trans)national Tsinoy body that encompasses Chinese, Filipino, and U.S. American identities. It is difficult to stand in front of everyone taking an oath to renounce my association with the country where I was born and raised. Like Eguchi's experience (Eguchi & Baig, 2018), "I cannot easily erase, ignore, and dismiss my past" (p. 43).

As soon as the oath ceremony is over, USCIS officials walk around the aisles of the convention center to direct participants to pick up their naturalization certificates. I follow the direction of the foot traffic towards where we first checked in, but this time a specific number was assigned to each person to pick up the certificate. I line up in front of Table 109 until the USCIS official calls my name. I step forward as instructed and give my form and permanent residency card. She glances at my form and permanent residency card to make sure I am the right person claiming my naturalization certificate. While waiting patiently, I cannot keep my eyes off the permanent residency card in which I will have to surrender; it is, after all, a symbol of my (trans)national hybridity as a Filipino national who has been a permanent resident of the United States. The USCIS official finds my certificate and checks its accompanying photo. She hands me the certificate and says enthusiastically, "Congratulations!" "Thank you," I say to her with a smile. I feel relieved and happy knowing I am officially a U.S. citizen. At the same time, I also know I have lost a part of me today as a Filipino national. I thought I had prepared myself for this moment, but I did not anticipate the feeling of identity loss would hit me this hard emotionally.

I walk away slowly from the USCIS official while holding my naturalization certificate tightly. The significance of the certificate represents my 23-year journey to becoming a U.S. citizen. The certificate also certifies my U.S. American identity that is recognized by the U.S. government. As Yep (2002) states, identity is one's self-concept based on "a particular social, geographical, cultural, and political context" (p. 61). My self-concept of the U.S. American identity has always been a part of me while living in the United States socially and culturally; however, it was difficult for me to legitimize my U.S. American identity as a Filipino citizen. Citizenship, after all, is often tied to nationality that has specific geographical and political constraints, especially when traveling (trans)nationally. As an example, I traveled to the Philippines again in 2011 with a Philippine passport. While preparing to place my belongings in a rectangular container bin for security check at the Los Angeles International Airport, the Transportation Security Administration (TSA) agent inspected my passport, smiled, and greeted me in accented Tagalog: "*Mabuhay! Kamusta na?*" ["How are you?"] (Hao, 2020). I was caught off guard, but I smiled back as a nonverbal confirmation that I understood his message. Even though the TSA agent validated the Philippines as my home, I believe he also read my body as Filipino based solely on my Philippine passport. Taking place in Los Angeles, which I consider home, my interaction with the TSA agent demonstrates my belongingness can be determined by documents like passports. My experience at the airport attests to the power of passports for potentially freezing identities (Cupach & Imahori, 1993) by marking bodies as local or foreign. In fact, passports and racial categorizations are intricately connected to communicate how one could be marked symbolically and materially (Drzewiecka & Steyn, 2012). Because the TSA agent's use of my passport to categorize me merely as a Filipino national, diverse cultural groups, such as (trans)national Tsina/oys, could be treated as "homogenous and static collectives" (Halualani et al., 2009, p. 21).

Like passports, U.S. naturalization certificates are used to document bodies as U.S. Americans. Having gone through the application process and attended the Oath of Allegiance ceremony, I am ecstatic to be holding my naturalization certificate. Looking down at the document closely, I immediately see "Certificate of Naturalization" printed on top and my full name listed correctly. I also examine the country of my former nationality: the Philippines. It is official that the Philippines is now known as my *former* nationality. Like other "imposed government identifications," naturalization certificates are "documents [that] constantly remind me of the dualities that reside within me" (Eguchi & Baig, 2018, p. 44). Although I am happy to be a U.S. citizen, the absence of my Filipino national identity confirms why (trans)national hybrid identities are never complete (Anthias, 2001) because the naturalization certificate, along with the oath I had taken, declare that I am officially a U.S. citizen and should not have any other national affiliation.

Embracing Tsinoy American Identity

The oath ceremony has finally concluded. Everyone who attended the ceremony dispersed in different directions. Many naturalized citizens pose for pictures in front of the gigantic U.S. flag at the convention center. I can see the festive nature of the oath ceremony's aftermath wherever I turn—one that resembles a high school or college commencement where family and friends gather to celebrate their loved one's momentous accomplishment. Instead of diplomas, naturalized citizens hold their naturalization certificates proudly. Strolling along the convention halls, I continue to follow the exit sign that directs me to the ground floor. Immediately after getting off the escalator, I see a foam board on a tripod greeting me boldly: "NEW CITIZEN BEAR." Right below it, a picture of a brown teddy bear holding a heart-shaped U.S. flag, which is followed by the message: "Tagged with Today's Date!" As I walk further down, I see a booth with a bright yellow banner indicating the sale of naturalization certificate covers for $10. Towards my left, I see a booth with a poster in front: "New U.S. Citizens Need Flowers!" Behind that same booth, a human-sized cutout of President Obama is visibly present smiling at passersby.

Upon exiting the convention center building, I spot a red banner at the top of a tent informing me to get memory photos. At the same location, I notice a long line of people waiting for a turn to get their photos taken with a backdrop of stars and stripes as a memento of this special day. Unlike other new naturalized citizens, I do not find it particularly exciting to take special photos and own memorabilia to remember the day I became a U.S. citizen. Perhaps my (trans)national embodied resistance communicates my tension of gaining, yet losing, a national identity. As I walk towards the parking lot, an elderly woman's patriotic look catches my attention; she dons a red flower hair clip, white shirt, and blue skirt to mark today's occasion. Moreover, her upbeat presence is evident for hopping around the sunbaked concrete floor while holding a family member's hand. She is the epitome of what the day of becoming a U.S. citizen is all about. While I do not know her specific life experiences, today commemorates her long journey (along with me and others) of becoming a U.S. citizen that many immigrants can only dream about. As McIntosh et al. (2020) point out, U.S. citizenship is often equated to U.S. Americanness, which centers whiteness as a discursive performance of universality. For many immigrants, the universal appeal of gaining U.S. citizenship is to engage in and, ultimately, achieve the white "American Dream."

After driving in the middle of Los Angeles rush hour traffic, I arrive home a little over an hour later. Dropping off my documents on the dining table, I rush to sit on the couch. Sitting comfortably, I call my brother, who also went through the naturalization process recently. Picking up the phone almost immediately, I share the good news with my brother for completing the oath ceremony, but I also talk about the tension I have been feeling all day. More specifically, I feel like I have gained and lost a part of me, which makes me "recognize the materiality of a border" (Eguchi & Baig, 2018, p. 43). As an empathetic listener, my brother comforts me with an understanding of our (trans)national identities as "conditions and contradictions of, and within, the nation intersect with the global, and vice-versa" (Shome & Hegde, 2002, p. 174). As someone who identifies as a (trans)national Tsinoy, I find it difficult to simply make a choice of which country I should belong to. After all, my body is always "caught up at the intersection of multiple, sometimes, conflicting, subject positions" (Shi, 2005, p. 55). I acknowledge that I am always at the intersection of contradictory embodiments as a Chinese, Filipino, and U.S. American. After attending the Oath of Allegiance ceremony today, my tensive experience prompts me to start considering what it means to have multiple identities and homes.

Coming back to Manila made me understand the connection between my *balikbayan* identity and cultural reentry. I critiqued much of the cultural reentry literature that tends to emphasize the home/host binary, which is problematic for those who have multiple cultural homes. Therefore, it is imperative to consider cultural returnees' identities from a "multi-dimensional view" for their changing, fragmentary, and contradictory nature (Kanno, 2000, p. 3). As Chang (2010) attests, "What happens during reentry are complicated processes of relating between people with many different identities" (p. 179). Traveling to the Philippines as a *balikbayan* reinforced the significance of reframing cultural reentry that can happen on a temporary, short-term basis. Moreover, my cultural reentries to the Philippines confirmed that my (trans)national Tsinoy body is not limited to one location but situates itself in political, historical, and contextual "performance[s] of coming home" (Eguchi & Baig, 2018, p. 45).

After speaking with my brother, I walk to the bedroom and stare at the picture of my spouse and son. The tension I have been feeling all day has subsided considerably. Seeing my family's faces inside of a 4" × 6" picture frame reminds of why I had applied for the U.S. citizenship in the first place, and, for that, I do not regret my decision to become a U.S. citizen. Losing my Filipino national identity in order to gain U.S. citizenship proved to be challenging emotionally, but I had to do it for my family to secure our future together in the United States. Even though my Filipino national identity is no longer official on paper, I recognize that my (trans)national hybridity as a Tsinoy American communicates my "new form of identity" (Young, 2009, p. 141). No matter what the documents say about me, one thing is for sure: I will always have my Chinese, Filipino, and U.S. American identities wherever I go. Perhaps that's what it means to be a *balikbayan*: in my case, a Tsinoy American who embodies my (trans)national hybridity and comes home to Manila and Los Angeles.

After becoming a naturalized U.S. citizen, I take the subsequent step of applying for a U.S. passport. Going through the application process means that I will be using a U.S. passport the next time I travel abroad. The passport application process is less complex than applying for citizenship. Within two weeks of my application, my U.S. passport arrives in a Priority Mail white envelope. Upon opening the envelope, I see the familiar navy-blue passport booklet. I review the second page carefully containing all my personal information. As I go down line by line, I see my surname and given name—both of which are spelled correctly. Then, I see my nationality: "United States of America." I take a slight pause realizing that the passport, along with my naturalization certificate, verifies I am a U.S. citizen. As I continue to read through the rest of the passport, I notice the Philippines is listed as my place of birth. I am delighted to see that my Filipino identity is listed explicitly to remind me of where I came from and why I am a Tsinoy American.

While the passport legitimizes my Tsinoyness, I believe it may also have unintended cultural consequences. After all, U.S. American identity has long been considered homogenous that is "particularly an unhyphenated one" (Kibria, 2000, p. 91), which is conflated with white identity (p. 94). For instance, listing the Philippines as my birthplace in the passport could also be used to distinguish me as Other from U.S.-born citizens. Airport officials who inspect my passport while traveling may notice that I was born outside of the United States, which could result in categorizing my body as a perpetual foreigner. As Sarup (1996) notes, identities tend to be constructed as "coherent, unified, [and] fixed" within specific cultural environments (p. 14), such as being able to distinguish who are natural-born and naturalized U.S. citizens. Therefore, a passport serves as a powerful—but contradicting—document that recognizes my (trans)national hybridity, yet it could also be used to categorize my otherness.

After examining my first U.S. passport, I put it away along with my expired Philippine passports in the same drawer. I feel nostalgic looking through every printed and stamped page in these documents. They remind me of specific moments as a child, teenager, and adult moving and traveling between the Philippines and the United States. Now owning a U.S. passport, I wonder what it would feel like to travel to the Philippines as a U.S. citizen. As I continue to travel between Manila and Los Angeles, I seek to experience how each home carries a special meaning for me personally, historically, socially, culturally, and politically. Having lived in the Philippines and the United States, both places have informed me of my evolvement as a Tsinoy American. Calling myself "Tsinoy American" represents my collective identities as Chinese, Filipino, and

U.S. American, but, more importantly, it communicates my *balikbayan* identity that can find its way home (trans)nationally.

References

Adler, N. J. (1981). Re-entry: Managing cross-cultural transitions. *Group and Organization Studies*, 6(3), 341–356. https://doi.org/10.1177/105960118100600310

Allen, C. (2016, February 19). Vatican: Pope's comments on Trump not "personal attack." *USA Today*. https://www.usatoday.com/story/news/politics/onpolitics/2016/02/19/pope-donald-trump-vatican/80622288/

Anderson, B. (1983). *Imagined communities: Reflections on the origin and spread of nationalism.* Verso.

Anthias, F. (2001). New hybridities, old concepts: The limits of "culture." *Ethnic and Racial Studies*, 24(4), 619–641. https://doi.org/10.1080/01419870120049815

Barro, J. (2015, December 15). How unpopular is Trump's Muslim ban? Depends how you ask. *New York Times*. https://www.nytimes.com/2015/12/16/upshot/how-unpopular-is-trumps-muslim-ban-depends-how-you-ask.html?_r=1&referer=

Berry, J. (1999). Intercultural relations in plural societies. *Canadian Psychology*, 40(1), 12–21. https://doi.org/10.1037/h0086823

Black, J. S., Gregersen, H. B., & Merdenhall, M. E. (1992). *Global assignments: Successfully expatriating and repatriating international managers.* Jossey-Bass.

Blanc, C. S. (1996). Balikbayan: A Filipino extension of the national imaginary and of state boundaries. *Philippine Sociological Review*, 44(1–4), 178–193. http://www.jstor.org/stable/41853680

Brabant, S., Palmer, C. E., & Gramling, R. (1990). Returning home: An empirical investigation of cross-cultural re-entry. *International Journal of Intercultural Relations*, 14(4), 387–404. https://doi.org/10.1016/0147-1767(90)90027-T

Chang, Y. Y. (2010). Are you my guest of my child? Mothers' uncertainties in interacting with their returnee children in China. *Chinese Journal of Communication*, 3(2), 167–184. https://doi.org/10.1080/17544751003740367

Clifford, J. (1992). Traveling cultures. In L. Grossberg, C. Nelson & P. Treichler (Eds.), *Cultural studies* (pp. 96–116). Routledge.

Cupach, W. R., & Imahori, T. T. (1993). Identity management theory: Communication competence in intercultural episodes and relationships. In R. L. Wiseman & J. Koester (Eds.), *Intercultural communication competence* (pp. 112–131). SAGE.

Drzewiecka, J. A., & Steyn, M. (2012). Racial immigrant incorporation: Material-symbolic articulation of identities. *Journal of International & Intercultural Communication*, 5(1), 1–19. https://doi.org/10.1080/17513057.2011.627093

Durham, M. G. (2004). Constructing the "new ethnicities": Media, sexuality, and diaspora identity in the lives of South Asian immigrant girls. *Critical Studies in Media Communication*, 21(2), 140–161. https://doi.org/10.1080/07393180410001688047

Eguchi, S., & Baig, N. (2018) Examining embodied struggles in cultural reentry through intersectional reflexivity. *Howard Journal of Communications, 29*(1), 33–48. https://doi.org/10.1080/10646175.2017.1315692

English Oxford Living Dictionaries. (2016, October 15). Balikbayan. http://www.oxforddictionaries.com/us/definition/american_english/balikbayan

Flores, L. A., & Gomez, L. R. (2020). Nightmares of whiteness: Dreams and deportability in the age of Trump. In D. M. D. McIntosh, D. G. Moon, & T. K. Nakayama (Eds.), *Interrogating the communicative power of whiteness* (pp. 198–217). Routledge. https://doi.org/10.4324/9780203730003

Gama, E., & Pedersen, P. (1977). Readjustment problems of Brazilian returnees from graduate studies in the United States. *International Journal of Intercultural Adjustment, 1*(4), 46–59. https://doi.org/10.1016/0147-1767(77)90031-1

Hall, S. (1996). Introduction: Who needs identity? In S. Hall & P. du Gay (Eds.), *Questions of cultural identity* (pp. 1–17). SAGE.

Halualani, R. T. (2008). "Where exactly is the Pacific?": Global migrations, diasporic movements, and intercultural communication. *Journal of International and Intercultural Communication, 1*(1), 3–22. https://doi.org/10.1080/17513050701739509

Halualani, R. T., Mendoza, S. L., & Drzewiecka, J. A. (2009). "Critical" junctures in intercultural communication studies: A review. *The Review of Communication, 9*(1), 17–35. https://doi.org/10.1080/15358590802169504

Hao, R. N. (2012). Cultural reentry: A critical review of intercultural communication research. In N. Bardhan & M. P. Orbe (Eds.), *Identity research and communication: Intercultural Reflections and Future Directions* (pp. 71–85). Lexington Books.

Hao, R. N. (2020). Critical intercultural performance framework: Transnational hybridity as performance of reentries. *Journal of Intercultural Communication Research, 49*(5), 425–432. https://doi.org/10.1080/17475759.2020.1798804

Harvey, M. G. (1989). Repatriation of corporate executives: An empirical study. *Journal of International Business Studies, 20*(1), 131–144. http://www.jstor.org/stable/154796

hooks, b. (1994). Homeplace: A site of resistance. In D. S. Madison (Ed.), *The woman that I am: The literature and culture of contemporary women of color* (pp. 448–454). St. Martin's.

Kanno, Y. (2000). Bilingualism and identity: The stories of Japanese returnees. *International Journal of Bilingual Education and Bilingualism, 3*(1), 1–17. https://doi.org/10.1080/13670050008667697

Kibria, N. (2000). Race, ethnic options, and ethnic binds: Identity negotiations of second-generation Chinese and Korean Americans. *Sociological Perspectives, 43*(1), 77–95. https://doi.org/10.2307/1389783

Kim, Y. Y. (2000). *Becoming intercultural: An integrative theory of communication and cross-cultural adaptation*. SAGE.

Kim, Y. Y. (2002). Cross-cultural adaptation: An integrative theory. In J. M. Martin, T. K. Nakayama, & L. A. Flores (Eds.), *Readings in cultural contexts* (2nd ed., pp. 237–245). Mc-Graw-Hill.

Kinefuchi, E. (2010). Finding home in migration: Montagnard refugees and post-migration identity. *Journal of International and Intercultural Communication*, 3(3), 228–248. https://doi.org/10.1080/17513057.2010.487220

Martin, J. N. (1984). The intercultural re-entry: Conceptualization and directions for future research. *International Journal of Intercultural Relations*, 8(2), 115–134. https://doi.org/10.1016/0147-1767(84)90035-X

Martin, J. N. (1986). Communication in the intercultural reentry: Student sojourners' perceptions of change in reentry relationships. *International Journal of Intercultural Relations*, 10(1), 1–22. https://doi.org/10.1016/0147-1767(86)90031-3

McIntosh, D. M. D., Moon, D. G., & Nakayama, T. K. (2020). Introduction: Introducing twenty-first century whiteness or "Everything old is new again." In D. M. D. McIntosh, D. G. Moon, & T. K. Nakayama (Eds.), *Interrogating the communicative power of whiteness* (pp. 1–12). Routledge. https://doi.org/10.4324/9780203730003

Rogers, J., & Ward, C. (1993). Expectation experience discrepancies and psychological adjustment during cross-cultural reentry. *International Journal of Intercultural Relations*, 17(2), 185–196. https://doi.org/10.1016/0147-1767(93)90024-3

Rohrlich, B. I., & Martin, J. N. (1991). Host country and reentry adjustment of student sojourners. *International Journal of Intercultural Relations*, 15(2), 163–182. https://doi.org/10.1016/0147-1767(91)90027-E

Sarup, M. (1996). *Identity, culture and the postmodern world*. University of Georgia Press.

Shi, Y. (2005). Identity construction of the Chinese diaspora, ethnic media use, community formation, and the possibility of social activism. *Continuum: Journal of Media & Cultural Studies*, 19(1), 55–72. https://doi.org/10.1080/1030431052000336298

Shome, R., & Hegde, R. S. (2002). Culture, communication, and the challenge of globalization. *Critical Studies in Media Communication*, 19(2), 172–189. https://doi.org/10.1080/07393180216560

Simmel, G. (1950). The stranger. In W. Hurt (Trans.), *The sociology of George Simmel* (pp. 402–408). The Free Press.

Smith, S. (2001). An identity model of reentry communication competence. *World Communication*, 30(3/4), 6–38.

Tomlin, C. R., Miller, M. L., Schellhase, E., New, G., Karwa, R., & Ouma, M. N. (2014). Assessing reverse culture shock following an international pharmacy practice experience. *Currents in Pharmacy Teaching and Learning*, 6(1), 106–113. https://doi.org/10.1016/j.cptl.2013.09.015

U.S. Citizenship and Immigration Services. (2020, April 23). *History of the Oath of Allegiance*. https://www.uscis.gov/citizenship/learn-about-citizenship/the-naturalization-interview-and-test/history-of-the-oath-of-allegiance

Wilson, A. H. (1993). A cross-national perspective on reentry of high school exchange students. *International Journal of Intercultural Relations*, 17(4), 465–492. https://doi.org/10.1016/0147-1767(93)90005-S

Yep, G. A. (2002). My three cultures: Navigating the multicultural identity landscape. In J. Martin, T. Nakayama, & L. Flores (Eds.), *Readings in intercultural communication: Experiences and contexts* (2nd ed., pp. 60–66). McGraw-Hill.

Young, S. L. (2009). Half and half: An (auto)ethnography of hybrid identities in a Korean American mother-daughter relationship. *Journal of International and Intercultural Communication, 2*(2), 139–167. https://doi.org/10.1080/17513050902759512

VIRTUALLY TSINA/OY: PERFORMING HYBRIDITY ONLINE

January 28, 2007. It is my second year of doctoral studies, and I am starting to settle into my new academic community. I have made new friends and gotten to know my professors. However, it has proven to be challenging for me culturally to live in a small college town of Carbondale, Illinois. Despite its natural beauty, Carbondale's rural Midwestern environment does not mirror my cultural being. I have been missing the presence of people who look and speak like me, foods that match my palate, and cultural practices that celebrate my (trans)national hybridity. To not see anything that reminds me of home in Los Angeles and Manila has made me especially long for a Tsina/oy community. With the absence of Tsina/oy community in Carbondale, I turn to the Internet and discover Tsinoy.com, an online community for Tsina/oys to (re)connect with their Chinese and Filipina/o identities.

Although no longer available as of June 20, 2011, Tsinoy.com provided several discussion forums concerning Tsina/oys—from Tsina/oy identity to popular culture to food to cultural/linguistic practices, among others (Hao, 2013). Many (trans)national hybrids turn to virtual communities like Tsinoy.com as places of belonging to search for news, to comment on cultural and political issues, and to negotiate their identities (Wenjing, 2005). In essence, electronic media, such as the Internet, have given (trans)national hybrids opportunities to construct their hybridized and fragmented cultural identities (Appadurai, 1996). Because Tsina/oys can engage in constitutive discourse about their "various traveling transnational subjectivities" online (Gajjala, 2004, p. 65), I argue Tsinoy.com functioned as a (trans)national space to challenge nationhood and citizenship (Basch et al., 1995) and offer "hybridity continuum" by communicating intersectional identities (Levitt & Jaworsky, 2007, p. 139).

By using cyberethnography, I seek to investigate how Tsinoy.com members performed their (trans)national Tsina/oy identity in a "virtual imagined communit[y]" (Gajjala, 2004, p. 13). I first discuss how Tsinoy.com members conceptualized Tsina/oyness as ethnic and (trans)national identities. I also examine Tsinoy.com members' performance of Tsina/oy identity through linguistic and cultural practices. I conclude the chapter with an analysis of how Tsina/oys used the online space to (re)define Tsina/oyness while experiencing multiple tensions.

Performing and Negotiating Tsina/oyness Online

February 19, 2007. I log onto Tsinoy.com as a cyberethnographer for the first time today. As a new participant here, I am slightly overwhelmed for not knowing exactly what to do and how to interact online. I had never been a participant in any online discussion forum before until now. Although I am ecstatic for finding a Tsina/oy online community, I feel nervous about observing and responding to discussion forum posts. In the midst of my anxiety, I proceed to look around the Web page. Forum after forum, members have posted and discussed many topics of interest to Tsina/oys that range from popular culture to foods to politics to anything in between. However, the *"Tsinoy Nga!"* ("Tsinoy Really!") discussion forum catches my eye. There is something about the expression of *"Tsinoy Nga!"* that intrigues me. I click on the discussion forum without hesitation and can tell right away that many enthusiastic members have engaged in lively conversations.

Tsina/oyness as Ethnic and (Trans)National Identities

With discussions taking place online, Tsinoy.com was a virtual community with members from the Philippines, China, Singapore, South Korea, Japan, Lebanon, Taiwan, Australia, England, Canada, the United States, among other countries. The diversity of Tsinoy.com members truly represented the established connection among them as a (trans)national online community to express their understanding of Tsina/oyness based on bloodlines, cultural influences, feelings, and in-group perception. A Tsinoy.com member, Brett, considered Tsina/oy as "someone whose ancestors are from China...and born and raised in the Philippines. Chinese by blood (heart and mind) but adapted to the Filipino way of life in addition to knowing (and practicing) the Chinese culture." Tsinoy.com members generally supported Brett's definition of "Tsina/oy" because Tsina/oyness as "nationalism is maintained through a sharing of beliefs and symbolic constructs as much as through geographical alliances and communal identities" (Flores & Hasian, 1997, p. 48).

Furthermore, other Tsina/oys declared that one's Tsina/oyness can also be determined based on surname and in-group perception. In many ways, Tsinoy.com was a space where Tsina/oys could (re)define Tsina/oyness and (re)connect with their identities. For instance, Sodoku asked the forum about their identity:

> I am confused if I am Tsinoy...At least that's what my last name (Ongjoco) tells me. I don't really look Chinese...I don't speak Fukien or Mandarin, or even Cantonese. But I have quite a few Chinese friends. My dad tells me that his grandfather is 50 percent Chinese, but that's just stories, I have not really traced my roots. Maybe someone here can enlighten me.

Sodoku's question is legitimate in terms of how identity is often tied to bloodlines. As someone who is only one-eighth Chinese, Sodoku was not sure about their Tsina/oy identity. Anthias (2001) explains, ethnic bonds are used as "the centrality of origin" (p. 632). However, if someone is less than 50% of something, does that affect their claim of being a part of a cultural group? Halo responded to Sodoku with the following statement:

> You may have a Chinese surname and have Chinese friends, but that doesn't really prove anything. Likewise, you may have Chinese blood and friends, but do you consider yourself Tsinoy? Or do you find that Filipino or Chinese FEELS stronger? I am not saying that you are one or the other, but I am saying that you should see what, exactly, you feel like. And that's what you are. Being Chinese or Filipino just by blood is not something you have to choose. It's by how close you are to each side.

According to Halo, a person's Tsina/oyness is not based on bloodlines; rather, Tsina/oyness is about one's connection or feeling of identity. Based on Sodoku and Halo's conversation, I posit Tsinoy.com allowed its participants to realize that Tsina/oyness could be defined by different factors, such as ancestry, location, shared beliefs, symbolic constructs, and feelings.

Although there are different ways to establish one's Tsina/oyness, Toyo determined that Sodoku is Tsina/oy by surname alone. Toyo responded with some historical information to Sodoku:

> The fact is that your surname is similar from the Chinese surname Ong, but when the Spaniards colonized Philippines the first Chinese settlers had to change or add some letters from their last name so that the Spaniards can pronounce their surname.

Toyo's response to Sodoku shows the complexity of Tsina/oyness, especially given the Spanish and U.S. colonization of the Philippines. Feiji agreed with Toyo and added that many Tsina/oys altered their surnames in order to own lands and properties during the Spanish colonization of the Philippines. Toyo and Feiji's remarks also confirmed that Tsina/oyness has multiple historicities that shape its meaning, such as Tsina/oyness can be understood based on how colonial and postcolonial subjects adopt identities as a result of colonization (Fanon, 1986).

In addition to bloodlines, cultural influences, and one's feelings or attitudes toward Tsina/oyness, a person's Tsina/oyness can also be determined based on in-group perception. One's in-group status can be understood as "identification with and perceived acceptance into a group that has shared systems of symbols and meanings as well as norms/rules for conduct" (Collier & Thomas, 1988, p. 113). Consequently, some Tsina/oys online struggled to call or identify themselves as Tsina/oy. Feiji, for example, voiced the following in the forum:

> Sometimes I think that to be considered a Tsinoy depends a lot on whether other people perceive you to be one. I mean, there are obvious traits of being Chinese... If people don't see the obvious traits, I doubt they'll see you as a Tsinoy, even though you think so otherwise.

Feiji reflected on how one's claim to a certain identity can be based on someone else's perception. The distinction of who is part of the in-group vs. outgroup on Tsinoy.com was evident. For example, Maple created a list of criteria of what constitutes a "Tsina/oy": "I can say anyone who was born in the Philippines and who knows how to speak both Chinese and Tagalog can be considered a Tsinoy." Maple's criteria for Tsina/oyness can easily be categorized through national origin and language acquisition. Maple's criteria are by no means comprehensive, as other online members had their own understandings of Tsina/oy identity. In a sense, a person's perceived "authenticity" matters in order to be considered as part of the in-group or out-group, which is a way for people to distinguish who is culturally similar or different in order to establish solidarity (Appiah, 1996).

The discussion of what Tsina/oyness means also resulted in some Tsinoy.com members privileging their Chinese or Filipina/o identity, which shows the differences in understanding of "Tsina/oy" because "the meanings of memories and symbols usually vary for different individuals and subgroups" (Georgiou, 2006, p. 40). Does "Tsina/oy" mean "Chinese Filipina/o," "Filipina/o Chinese," or something else? To define Tsina/oyness, Cutiepie wrote about the difference between "Chinese Filipina/o" and "Filipina/o Chinese":

> "Filipino-Chinese" refers to the traditional or older Chinese who are predominantly Chinese in identity but Filipino in citizenship...."Chinese Filipino" refers to the young, mostly native-born ethnic Chinese who identify themselves as Filipinos first, but still maintain their Chinese cultural identity.

Cutiepie defined "Chinese Filipino" and "Filipino Chinese" based on intergenerational gaps and their influences on what is privileged—ethnic or national identity. For Cutiepie, a "Filipino Chinese" is someone who privileges ethnic identity as Chinese, while a "Chinese Filipino" is the opposite. Since ethnic or national borders serve as key conditions for hybridity (Bhabha, 1994), many Tsina/oys like Cutiepie would consider Tsina/oyness based on ethnicity or national identity.

However, Halo could not agree with Cutiepie's differentiation of "Chinese Filipino" from "Filipino Chinese." Halo said, "I'd like to contest this. 'Chinese Filipinos' are people of Chinese descent, born in or naturalized to the Philippines. 'Filipino Chinese,' on the other hand, are people of Filipino descent, born in or naturalized to China." Halo's explanation seemed to be more logical and popular among Tsinoy.com participants than Cutiepie's perspective. Like Halo, Piggybank had a similar understanding of what "Chinese Filipino" and "Filipino Chinese" are: "Filipino-Chinese means Chinese living in the Philippines, while Chinese-Filipino pertains to Filipinos with Chinese ancestry. Chinese Filipinos are born in the Philippines having a Filipino citizenship."

Many Tsinoy.com members seemed to agree that Tsina/oyness consists of both Chinese and Filipina/o backgrounds. Note how Worldtraveler, a Lebanese-Chinese born and raised in the Philippines, responded to my queries of whether he considers himself Tsinoy:

> Yes. I consider myself Tsinoy for the following reasons: A. Chinese: My mother is Chinese so that makes me Chinese as well. B. Filipino: Though not by blood, race and ethnicity, The Philippines is my home, my country. I was born and raised here (though I hold dual citizenship).

Worldtraveler's multicultural identity is another example of why Tsina/oyness is so complex; Tsina/oyness was communicated here not to reduce it in the literal sense (i.e., Chinese + Filipina/o = Tsina/oy), but, rather, to show that Tsina/oyness could be composed of ethnic, racial, and national identities. So, like Halo, Cutiepie, and Piggybank, Worldtraveler also conveyed that, in conjunction with his Lebanese identity, Tsinoyness is an identity that encompasses both Chinese and Filipino cultures to some degree.

Tsinoy.com members did not agree on one specific definition of "Tsina/oy." After all, (trans)national hybrid identities are never complete, which can also designate the formation of new identities that are transethnic and transnational in nature (Anthias, 2001). As a result, hybrid identities are "constantly producing and reproducing themselves anew, through transformation and difference" (Hall, 1990, p. 235). Tsina/oyness is not just about ethnic and national identity; it is a combination of different factors. Perhaps there was not a consensus on what "Tsina/oy" means because Tsinoy.com participants had different life experiences. Since Tsina/oyness cannot be defined succinctly, some Tsina/oys online defined their Tsina/oyness based on their immigrant status in the Philippines (i.e., Chinese national living in the Philippines), whereas others considered their Tsina/oyness due to their ethnicity. The presumed in-group membership in the Tsinoy.com community likely resulted in each participant defining Tsina/oyness in a way consistent with their own situation.

Tsina/oyness and Linguistic Performances

Tsina/oys who logged onto Tsinoy.com also performed and negotiated their (trans)national hybridity by using different languages when participating in online discussions. How Tsinoy.com members posted their messages online communicated identity and cultural politics that situated them as members of that community. Although English appeared to be the dominant language, Tagalog and Chinese (Hokkien, to be more specific) were also present, which reflected the participants' hybridity was "full of discontinuities and ruptures" (Anthias, 2001, p. 626), allowing them to write in different speech codes while interacting online. In essence, it was not unusual for Tsina/oys to post their messages in bilingual or trilingual (a combination of Tagalog, English, and Hokkien). For example, Castro wrote to me and Hulagirl:

> *Hwag na natin ituloy ang usapan* [Translation from Tagalog: Let's not continue this discussion]. *Pinoys* [Filipinos] will always look upon us as Chinese. Whether or not we are Tsinoys or *"bagong salta"/Tai-diyok'ah* [Translation from Tagalog/Hokkien: Whether or not we are Tsinoys or "newcomer"/from Mainland China].

Castro's message was posted in three languages, which is not uncommon for Tsina/oys due to the Philippines' diverse linguistic practices. Even though Tagalog and English are co-official languages of the Philippines, English tends to be used primarily in government and instruction. Therefore, a lot of Filipina/os and Tsina/oys speak Taglish (hybrid of Tagalog and English) (Thompson, 2003).

March 5, 2007. I notice that one of the discussion threads on language has generated a lot of responses from Tsinoy.com members. The thread "Daily Dose of Hokkien/Fukien" aims to provide Hokkien language lessons to those who want to learn a language that many Tsina/oys speak. Hokkien is a Chinese language that is a variant of Taiwanese that is also referred to as Fukien(ese) or Minnan (Juan, 2006). Seeing a topic on Hokkien being discussed in the forum resonates with me. For members to speak Hokkien reminds me of my childhood days in Manila when I used to speak it daily. Our similarity with multilingualism, especially communicating in Hokkien, bonds me instantly with the members of the community. I feel at home.

In addition to Tagalog and English, communicating in Hokkien is an important aspect of Tsina/oy identity. Halo reported the following news to the members:

> Taiwan...has released a list of 300 characters...that may be used to write out full sentences of Minnan (the Taiwanese variant, anyway) without the use of Romanization...Personally, while I'm glad that they are making Taiwanese more accessible to the general public through the propagation of a writing system.

Because most Tsina/oys speak Hokkien, in addition to English and Tagalog, Halo's news above said a lot about the importance of preserving Hokkien. Halo's remark about preserving Hokkien was a performance of Tsina/oy pride by connecting the linguistic importance of Hokkien to Tsina/oy identity. Halo continued by expressing concern for the Hokkien's endangered status: "You must keep in mind that this [Taiwan's effort to create characters to represent Minnan] was made to ensure that Hokkien as a dialect will not just die out." Because of Hokkien's endangered status, many Tsina/oys also wanted to (re)learn Hokkien by practicing phrases and words in pinyin-like writings (i.e., spelled out using the Latin alphabet). Tsina/oys who wanted to learn Hokkien used that opportunity to reconnect with their Tsina/oyness online and maintain one's ontological status (Yep, 2002).

Tsinoy.com members used the online space to reclaim their identities by incorporating Hokkien as part of the daily discourse (Hao, 2013). To promote linguistic preservation, Halo also expressed disgust for Tsina/oys who wanted to learn Mandarin because it is like forgetting Hokkien:

> I don't get it. The very thread says "Daily Dose of Hokkien/Fukien" and someone posts "I'm really interested in learning Mandarin" here? Madness. We should all exert effort to strive to learn Hokkien. C'mon people…leave Mandarin to the mainlanders. We're Hokkienese. We ought to be proud of it.

Halo's response would strike some Tsina/oys as anti-Mandarin rhetoric, but I can understand Halo's concerns. Learning Mandarin on a Tsina/oy Web site is like privileging another language over their own. If Tsinoy.com was an online community for Tsina/oys, then why did people want to learn Mandarin, a dominant Chinese language? As de Certeau (1984) points out, conforming to learn and master a language could reinforce who has power and is privileged:

> The mastery of language guarantees and isolates a new power, a "bourgeois" power, that of making history and fabricating languages. This power, which is essentially scriptural, challenges not only the privilege of "birth," that is, of the aristocracy, but also defines the code governing socioeconomic promotion and dominates, regulates, or selects according to its norms all those who do not possess this mastery of language. (p. 139)

In some ways, de Certeau's point resonates to Halo's concerns about conforming to master a dominant language from China (i.e., Mandarin) that essentially marginalizes Hokkien, a language that many Tsina/oys speak. Mandarin is a dominant Chinese language because of its demand in business settings, and as China continues its status as a global economic superpower, some Tsina/oys might find it more important to learn Mandarin than Hokkien.

Moreover, because Mandarin is the primary language spoken in China, many Tsina/oys online perceived that being able to speak Mandarin can make one "authentic Chinese." In fact, Halo told me the following:

> Yes, this is the common (almost ubiquitous) misconception. When Tsinoys refer to "Chinese," they always mean Mandarin, and "Hokkien/Minnan" is just the "dialect."

It's rather sad, really. And there's this horrendous misconception that someone is "higher" or more educated if they speak Mandarin.

Thinking about de Certeau's point, learning how to speak Mandarin fluently could allow Tsina/oys not only to earn economic but also social and cultural power. Interestingly, there were Tsina/oys who resisted Mandarin as a primary means of communication by stating their interest in learning Hokkien:

JEFF: Anyway, I really need to learn Fookien [Hokkien], coz my closest friend is pure Chinese (and yes, she speaks Fookien [Hokkien]).

CLOUDNINE: I went to Chinese school way back in my elementary years, not even a year though. That was hard for me then to write Chinese characters. Somehow, I realized, if I have pursued it, maybe I'm fluent and good at it now.

Jeff and Cloudnine's resistance to Mandarin can be demonstrated by showing genuine interest in learning how to speak Hokkien. To take it a step further, one's opposition to Mandarin could be enacted by posting messages explicitly in Hokkien. For instance, right after Halo expressed disgust for Tsina/oys wanting to learn Mandarin, Joe Black immediately posted a part of his message in Hokkien communicating his interest in learning the language: "My dad's Chinese, yet we don't use it as our primary tongue. I understand, but cannot speak fluently.....*gua ehiaw kong tampo lang nang we*" [Translation from Hokkien: "I know how to speak a little Hokkien"]. Writing in Hokkien, Joe Black legitimized Hokkien as an important language to learn. Pat responded to Joe Black to offer support for helping him learn Hokkien. Pat said, "Hi joeblack, I can help you. Let me know what you want to learn and I will try to answer what I can." Some Tsina/oys like Cloudnine, Halo, Jeff, Joe Black, and Pat made their point that Hokkien is as Chinese as Mandarin by starting a thread and engaging in conversations that would help communicate the importance of preserving it.

Tsina/oy Cultural Traditions and Practices

February 20, 2007. Two days after the Lunar New Year, I visit Tsinoy.com. The holiday spirit is in full swing in the forum based on the abundance of online posts and replies concerning how Tsina/oys celebrate the new year (e.g., types of rituals, foods, etc.). Tsinoy.com members reaffirm their enthusiasm by sharing personal stories of following and modifying Lunar New Year traditions in (trans)national spaces. As a (trans)national Tsinoy in the United States,

I empathize with Tsina/oys who could not celebrate Lunar New Year extensively. Even though members vary in ways of celebrating the new year, I can see many posts reflecting similar practices among us that help maintain our Tsina/oyness.

Tsinoy.com served as a forum for its members to communicate their Tsina/oy identity by sharing different cultural traditions and practices like the Lunar New Year. According to Sarup (1996), identity is a social construction that connects between people, institutions, and practices. Given their (trans)national hybrid identity, most Tsina/oys tend to celebrate traditions in their own unique ways. Unicorn and Aurora shared the following:

UNICORN: I remember back home we used to do this [ritual] before the new year: get 12 circular fruits, coins in our pockets, my mom (every year) and dad put lots of coins under their bed. We also jump at midnight (so we can grow taller).

AURORA: *Ginagawa ko din yan dati nung mga 12 years old, pero talaga hanggang 5'3" lang ang kaya ng buto ko pataasin ako* [Translation from Tagalog: I've been jumping since I was twelve years old, but my bones could only carry me through 5'3"].

No matter how silly or superstitious in nature, Tsina/oys, such as Unicorn and Aurora, engage in some variation of cultural practices they grew up with to maintain their Tsina/oyness. Rituals enacted during Lunar New Year solidify their understanding of Tsina/oy identity. Besides the jumping ritual, many Tsina/oys also celebrate the Lunar New Year with *ang pao* (red envelope). Aurora and Gloria discussed the importance of red envelopes; however, both admitted that they grew up in non-traditional Tsina/oy households. Gloria said, "*Hindi ko nakasanayan na magbigay or bigyan ng ang pao* because I grew up in a Filipino environment" [Translation from Tagalog: "I've never been accustomed to giving red envelopes because I grew up in a Filipino environment"]. Aurora agreed, "Gloria, *Sinabi mo*" [Translation from Tagalog: "Gloria, you said it"]. Since not all Tsinoy.com members appeared to follow traditional Chinese practices, such as giving or receiving red envelopes during Lunar New Year, they altered how it is celebrated. Altering but maintaining Chinese traditions and practices to fit the Tsina/oy lifestyle is what Gilroy calls "changing same," which refers to "the invention of tradition as much as to tradition itself" (cited in Hall, 1996, p. 4). To put it simply, "changing same" occurs when traditions are modified but continued at the same time. As Gilroy puts it, "changing same" is "not the so-called return to roots but a coming-to-terms-with our 'routes'" (p. 4).

In addition to Lunar New Year, Tsinoy.com members conversed about the celebration of the Mooncake Festival. The Mooncake Festival—also known as Mid-Autumn Festival—is held "on the fifteenth day of the eighth lunar month" (Roy, 2005, p. 282), which typically falls on September or October of the Gregorian (Western) calendar. Traditionally, Chinese families celebrate with a big feast that includes mooncakes. Mooncakes are pastries that normally include lotus seed paste and egg yolks. Kambing, Confucius, Toyo, Aurora, Bigas, and many other Tsina/oys revealed that they continue to eat mooncake to keep their Tsina/oy tradition alive.

It is also a well-known Tsina/oy tradition to play *Poah-tiong-chhiu* (dice game) to commemorate the Mooncake Festival. Mingtao provided a cultural context of the dice game:

> The dice game can only be found in Minnan area of Fujian and some overseas Chinese communities. Some people in Taiwan also play that game. Cantonese, Hakkas and people of other places do not play that game, that's why you will not find it in Hong Kong.

Because the dice game can be found in some of the overseas Chinese communities, Tsina/oys in the Philippines have incorporated the tradition as part of the Tsina/oy culture. The dice game is normally played with six dice that are thrown in a bowl, and whoever gets a specific set of numbers from the dice wins a prize. For instance, a dice combination with only one 4-face—1, 2, 3, 4, 5, and 6—wins the top prize (See, 2015). Other order of prize levels can be determined by the number of 4-faced die: two 4-faced dice, three 4-faced dice, etc. In sum, the fewer 4-faced die, the better. However, not every Tsina/oy family follows the same rule. As an example, Multiethnic described his family's dice game:

> When I was a child, we used to play with dices, the score that you will get is the equivalent to your prize, which is HOPIA [a Tsina/oy pastry]. The higher your score, the bigger your HOPIA is! Each member of the family is required to join, and the one who will get the biggest HOPIA will be lucky for that whole year!

As far as I can remember, the dice game has been a cultural tradition for Tsina/oys to celebrate the Mooncake Festival. The prize for the dice game varies from family to family. For Multiethnic's family, the prize was *hopia*. For Peklat, on the other hand, she won a "plant holder stand." In a way, the dice game operates in which hybridization acts as "the ways in which forms become separated from existing practices and recombine with new forms of new practices" (Rowe & Schelling, 1991, p. 231). Although the nature of the dice game has remained consistent, it has also evolved that makes it possible for (trans)national Tsina/oys to modify its prizes.

(Re)Defining Tsina/oyness Online

May 18, 2007. Learning about Tsina/oy cultural practices from Tsinoy.com members continues to remind me of home. I am happy to be back in Los Angeles with my family for the next few weeks after completing another year of graduate school. Staying in my parents' house has always reminded me of my Tsina/oyness—not only because of my Tsina/oy parents but also having access to Chinese and Filipina/o foods in the neighborhood. Like today, it is not unusual for me to walk to a local Filipina/o grocery store within a few blocks from my parents' house. After picking up a few Filipina/o dishes prepared and sold in the grocery store, I go to the checkout lane where a Filipina cashier greets me warmly. Paying for what I owe, I respond in Tagalog: "*Salamat*" ["Thank you"]. The cashier appears to be surprised by asking in Tagalog, "*Pilipino ka ba?*" ["Are you Filipino?"]. Grabbing my purchased bag of dishes, I respond with a big smile: "*Opo*" ["Yes"]. "No way!" the cashier exclaims in disbelief. "No, you're Chinese," she insists.

Like me and other (trans)national hybrids, Tsinoy.com members spoke about the need to perform their Chinese and Filipina/o identities in particular ways to be accepted by members of both Chinese and Filipina/o communities. Consequently, many of them expressed experiences of multiple tensions (Yep, 2002). For instance, Josie mentioned the following: "It's also hard because pure Filipinos would treat me as Chinese. However, most Chinese don't consider me as 'one of them.' Also, because I don't speak fluent Fookien." Josie commented what it is like to be in-between—a constant struggle to fit in due to a physical or linguistic marker. Like Josie, Gloria added her frustration for not being accepted as Chinese:

> I don't speak Chinese, but I'm 3/4 Chinese. My husband's family complains a lot about my being un-Chinese. I grew up in a Filipino culture and never studied Chinese. Aside from that, most of my friends are Filipinos...Everyone says that I'm more Filipino, maybe so. My blood will always be Chinese, even if I don't speak the language.

Because of her very limited exposure to Chinese culture and language, Gloria failed to legitimize her Chineseness. Gloria's testimonial reminds me of how

Anzaldúa (1999) wrote about how difficult it was for her to establish her Chicana identity due to constant negotiation when speaking Spanish and English in different contexts. Even though Anzaldúa's experience was different, Gloria faced similar obstacles in legitimizing her Tsinay identity because she lacks familiarity with the Chinese language. Gloria wanted to reclaim that part of her identity in order for others to accept her not only as a Filipina, but also as a Tsinay.

Jackie, who was born and raised in the Philippines, also noted about her and her friends' lack of Chineseness: "We're not as Chinese. We've become too Filipinonized." Due to their upbringing, Jackie elaborated that she and her friends speak mostly Tagalog and English. Although Jackie's narrative is an example of how the tension exists for having (trans)national hybrid identities, it is also an instance of how Tsina/oyness is linked to national identity (for being born and raised in the Philippines), which challenges the notion of Tsina/oyness being restricted to ethnic and linguistic backgrounds. Jackie claimed that she is not as Chinese as other Tsina/oys, but her post suggested how many Tsina/oys today do not necessarily have to prove they are "Chinese" to be considered Tsina/oy. According to Leeds-Hurwitz (2006), cultural identity is conveyed in a variety of ways from one generation to another, which is perhaps why Jackie's perceived lack of Chineseness—for being a generation or so removed from speaking Hokkien and practicing Chinese traditions—did not deter her from claiming her Tsinayness in her posts. Many Tsina/oys today could relate to Jackie's experience, especially younger ones, and believe that not learning how to speak Hokkien does not make them any less Tsina/oy because their national and ethnic identities could also mark their Tsina/oyness in other ways.

Although many Tsina/oys online described various tensions associated with their identities, some believed that participating in Tsinoy.com was an empowering experience for being able to celebrate their (trans)national hybridity. Perhaps these Tsina/oys realized that hybridity is not a liability but an asset. As Pascual (2004) says, hybridity is an "ongoing experience of two cultures as a legitimate process" (pp. 288–289). Instead of thinking that people should be ashamed of their hybrid identity, they should acknowledge it. Brett commented, "If my nationality is Filipino, I'd tell them I'm Filipino and would tell them my grandparents are from China though. So I consider myself as a Chinese-Filipino." Siopao agreed with Brett: "No matter what my elders say regarding being born Chinese, it doesn't hold any weight in the USA. Fusion is the way." Siopao's use of "fusion" suggested his acknowledgment of hybridity.

Because of globalization, images of culture are diverse, non-coherent, complex, interactive, and dynamic (Featherstone, 1995), which makes hybridity inevitable for people who are in-between due to their multicultural identities. As a result, limiting identity within nation and culture does not accurately portray people with mixed identities (Pascual, 2004). For instance, Singkit voiced concerns about identity categorization:

> Globalisation has made the definition of ethnicity and nationality difficult because we share so much (i.e., culture, food, music, etc.) with different people groups. The sad thing is, we still force to distinguish people according to ethnicity rather than according to who a person is.

From Singkit's point of view, hybrid identity is complex and political (Anzaldúa, 1999; Pascual, 2004). Perhaps that is why Appadurai (1996) suggests that "we need to think ourselves beyond the nation" (p. 158) because thinking about identity from the nation-state perspective "often create[s], revitalize[s], or fracture[s] ethnic identities that were previously fluid, negotiable, or nascent" (p. 162). In essence, those who resist categorizations will seek for alternatives and possibilities to challenge the dominant power (hooks, 1990). Tsinoy.com allowed its members to examine and (re)define what it means to be Tsina/oy.

Even though Tsina/oys live in many parts of the world, many still cling on to their Tsina/oy identity (Hao, 2013). After all, it is not unusual for (trans)national hybrids to "hold tight to their identities defined by the home-country nationalism or the 'traditional culture'" (Shi, 2005, p. 58). Augustin (1999) argues that online community members who are excluded from mainstream society are more likely to "see themselves as protagonists of the revolution" (p. 152) in which they can gain useful information, share their stories, and educate others. In particular, Tsinoy.com became a place where Tsina/oys supported each other, and they used it as a "home" space to claim their Tsina/oyness. For instance, I found a forum in which Aphrodite asked people whether she is a Tsinay, and others responded with support and confirmation:

APHRODITE: Hi guys, I'm new here. My grandfather in my mother's side is Fujianese, which makes me a quarter...So what do you guys think, am I considered Tsinoy? I'll tell you what I consider myself to be, after your replies.

AURORA: After analyzing your post for 2–3 minutes, I can say you are a Tsinoy.

UNICORN: I think you're a Tsinoy too. As long as you have that blood, it doesn't matter where you live. You're still a Tsinoy.

APHRODITE: Even though I was exposed more to Filipino culture than Chinese while growing up, I still managed to familiarize myself with certain aspects of

Tsinoy culture. We also celebrate 2 new years per year. One is Western new year, the other is Lunar new year...So what do I consider myself to be? Well, I am a Filipino-American of Tsinoy descent.

Like Aphrodite and Unicorn, Worldtraveler's Tsinoyness is embedded in his multiple identities, as he shared with me in the forum:

> Many are confused as to what race I come from. Some would say I possess some Chinese features at first glance though when they stare at me for a longer period, I look more of an Arab. Being introduced is a funny experience. My friends would usually tell people "here is our Lebanese-Chinese but Filipino by heart friend."

Hearing from Worldtraveler's perspective attests to what many of us have been feeling as (trans)national hybrids. His reply to my question in the discussion forum made me think about my own Tsinoyness. While we have unique experiences, I could relate with Worldtraveler in terms of how others read our bodies and how we respond to those cultural interpretations. As an example, many people I encounter would automatically assume I am Chinese, which is not completely inaccurate; however, when I identify as Tsinoy, they have a hard time conceptualizing my Filipino identity. As illustrated in other Tsinoy.com members' narratives, other Tsina/oys have faced similar challenges in negotiating their Tsina/oyness. To deal with multiple tensions, Tsinoy.com made it possible for its members to create sites of resistance to (re)define Tsina/oyness across (trans)national spaces.

Home Away from Home

October 24, 2007. I turn on my laptop to log onto Tsinoy.com once again like what I have been doing for the last eight months. However, today is the last official time for me to visit the site as a cyberethnographer. It is bittersweet to conclude my cyberethnography of Tsinoy.com, but I plan to continue to visit the community I have grown to love. After all, I have gotten to know some of the Tsina/oys in this community who have shared with me their own lives. Regardless of personal and cultural experiences, Tsina/oys here have created a sense of belonging for me and other (trans)national Tsina/oys worldwide. Because of all Tsinoy.com members involved, I have found a home away from home.

Tsinoy.com functioned as an online space to unite Tsina/oys and recognize that even though everyone's Tsina/oyness varies to some degree, they are still

Tsina/oy. In addition, the forum opened up discussions on what Tsina/oyness means. Tsina/oyness is not fixed but fluid: A person can claim a Tsina/oy identity based on ethnicity, nationality, culture, language, or traditions. In sum, Tsina/oyness, like other identities, evolves, grows, and changes. Even though some members of the forum pointed out that Tsina/oyness is synonymous to "Chinese Filipina/o" or "Filipina/o Chinese," not everyone can fit into the mold of either of these identity labels, which normally restricts Tsina/oyness as ethnicity or nationality. As a response, multicultural Tsina/oys used Tsinoy.com to challenge the meaning of Tsina/oy. Contestations about culture are part of exercising one's power (Bourdieu, 1990), especially when Tsina/oyness is often thought as adding Chinese and Filipina/o identities together. Worldtraveler clearly demonstrated in his post that his multicultural background may confuse others, but his Tsina/oy friends have accepted him as a Tsinoy. Perhaps Worldtraveler's friends thought of Tsinoyness as nonsummative, wherein an identity is not about adding different parts together (Cupach & Imahori, 1993). Rather, Tsina/oyness is also about a combination of experiences, values, beliefs, and perceptions in different cultures one may have (Yep, 2002). Therefore, Worldtraveler's online posts proved to be empowering, as the Web site itself can provide multiple belongings that dismantled the notion of a unitary identity. As Tsinoy.com participants came from all over the world, I have learned that Tsina/oyness is so much more beyond ethnic identity; it can also encompass linguistic and cultural practices, self-identification, in-group status, and connection to home.

Although many Tsina/oys could express their identity performances online, they are likely to continue to face multiple tensions because their "locational, spatial, and positional dilemma is heightened by the present events that surround" them (Chawla, 2003, p. 275). Due to their multicultural identities, some Tsina/oys may feel a lack of acceptance. Even though Tsina/oys online were generally supportive of each other, I noticed there were identity performances that appeared to have excluded multicultural Tsina/oys who did not fit the profile of a typical Tsina/oy. For some, "Tsina/oy" was limited to "Chinese Filipina/o" or "Filipina/o Chinese." Although such discourses did not specifically target specific multicultural Tsina/oys, such identity labels strategically erased (even if implicitly) them as part of the in-group. Responding to dominant discourses online, Worldtraveler suggested that Tsina/oyness should also be about one's connection to "home." Worldtraveler, a Lebanese-Chinese, classified himself as Tsinoy because the Philippines is his "home"—the place where he grew up and lives. In some ways, Worldtraveler discussed "home" to problematize Tsina/oyness and encourage us to think about it in another way.

Because Tsina/oys come from all walks of life, it is impossible to have a clear definition of who Tsina/oys are. Derived from Anzaldúa's (1999) notion of how identities are relative, I argue Tsina/oys whose first language is English or Tagalog can be just as much a Tsina/oy as one who speaks Arabic. A Tsina/oy from Malaysia is just as much a Tsina/oy as one from the Philippines. As Yep (2002) says, "Cultural identities are co-created and re-created in everyday interaction" (p. 63); therefore, Tsina/oyness will continue to be defined and re-defined. Because of transnational movements in which refugees, tourists, or students settle together in one place (Appadurai, 1996), collective cultural communities will continue to be established. As a result, someone who has a hyphenated identity will probably be twice hyphenated. In this case, Tsina/oys who live in the United States like me may appropriately call ourselves "Tsina/oy Americans."

I must also acknowledge that issues of technology and class could prevent some Tsina/oys from participating in Tsinoy.com (Hao, 2013). Given that Tsinoy.com was an online community, one must have technological and economic means to access the Internet. As Gajjala (2004) explains, "any kind of technology requires that we investigate issues that are much more complex than merely the question of material access to the latest technologies...[and] to understand the (dis)empowering potential of any particular technology and associated technological practices" (p. 40). Thus, Tsinoy.com participants were privileged in many ways (e.g., by class as well as technological literacy) to access and engage in the online community.

After participating in Tsinoy.com as a Tsinoy researcher for several months, I contend Tsinoy.com was a "home away from home" for Tsina/oys. According to Gajjala (2004), virtual and physical worlds are becoming inseparable, and people do, in fact, enact their social lives online. Like the physical spaces they inhabit, Tsina/oys around the world had another home online that created opportunities to reflect on how they could reconstruct their Tsina/oy subjectivities. Perhaps Sarup (1996) said it best: That home can be any place a person wants it to be—wherever the family is, where parents are buried, a place from which a person has been displaced, or even a place where a person is at the moment. For Tsina/oys who logged onto the Internet and accessed Tsinoy.com, the Web site became a "home" that provided possibilities to (re)claim their Tsina/oyness and be accepted for who they are.

References

Anthias, F. (2001). New hybridities, old concepts: The limits of "culture." *Ethnic and Racial Studies, 24*(4), 619–641. https://doi.org/10.1080/01419870120049815

Anzaldúa, G. (1999). *Borderlands/La Frontera: The new mestiza* (2nd ed.). Aunt Lute Books.

Appadurai, A. (1996). *Modernity at large: Cultural dimensions of globalization*. University of Minnesota Press.

Appiah, K. A. (1996). Identity: Political not cultural. In M. Garber, R. L. Walkowitz, & P. B. Franklin (Eds.), *Fieldwork: Sites in literary and cultural studies* (pp. 34–40). Routledge.

Augustin, L. (1999). They speak, but who listens? In W. Harcourt (Ed.), *Women@Internet: Creating new cultures in cyberspace* (pp. 149–155). Zed Press.

Basch, L., Glick Schiller, N., & Szanton Blanc, C. (1995). *Nations unbound. Transnational projects, postcolonial predicaments, and deterritorialized nation-states*. Gordon and Breach Publishers.

Bhabha, H. (1994). *The location of culture*. Routledge.

Bourdieu, P. (1990). *The logic of practice*. Polity.

Certeau, M. de (1984). *The practice of everyday life* (S. Rendall, Trans.). University of California Press.

Chawla, D. (2003). Rhythms of dis-location. In R. P. Clair (Ed.), *Expressions of ethnography: Novel approaches to qualitative methods* (pp. 271–280). State University of New York Press.

Collier, M. J., & Thomas, M. (1988). Cultural identity: An interpretive perspective. In Y. Y. Kim & W. B. Gudykunst (Eds.), *Theories in intercultural communication* (pp. 99–120). SAGE.

Cupach, W. R., & Imahori, T. T. (1993). Identity management theory: Communication competence in intercultural episodes and relationships. In R. L. Wiseman & J. Koester (Eds.), *Intercultural communication competence* (pp. 112–131). SAGE.

Fanon, F. (1986). *Black skin, white masks*. Pluto Press.

Featherstone, M. (1995). *Undoing culture: Globalization, postmodernity, and identity*. SAGE.

Flores, L. A., & Hasian, M. A. (1997). Returning to Aztlán and Laraza: Political communication and the vernacular construction of Chicano/a nationalism. In A. Gonzalez & D. V. Tanno (Eds.), *Politics, communication, and culture* (pp. 186–203). SAGE.

Gajjala, R. (2004). *Cyber selves: Feminist ethnographies of South Asian women*. AltaMira Press.

Georgiou, M. (2006). *Diaspora, identity and the media*. Hampton Press.

Hall, S. (1990). Cultural identity and diaspora. In J. Rutherford (Ed.), *Identity: Community, culture, & difference* (pp. 222–237). Lawrence & Wishart.

Hall, S. (1996). Introduction: Who needs identity? In S. Hall & P. du Gay (Eds.), *Questions of cultural identity* (pp. 1–17). SAGE.

Hao, R. N. (2013). Virtually Tsina/oy: Performing and negotiating diasporic hybridity online. *Qualitative Communication Research, 2*(2), 159–181. https://doi.org/10.1525/qcr.2013.2.2.159

hooks, b. (1990). *Yearning: Race, gender, and cultural politics*. South End Press.

Juan, G. B. (2006, May 3). Intercultural exchange is mutually beneficial. *The Manila Times*. https://www.manilatimes.net/2006/05/03/news/top-stories/intercultural-exchange-is-mutually-beneficial/800881

Leeds-Hurwitz, W. (2006). Introduction: Maintaining cultural identity over time. In W. Leeds-Hurwitz (Ed.), *From generation to generation: Maintaining cultural identity over time* (pp. 1–28). Hampton Press.

Levitt, P., & Jaworsky, B. N. (2007). Transnational migration studies: Past developments and future trends. *Annual Review of Sociology, 33*, 129–156. https://doi.org/10.1146/annurev.soc.33.040406.131816

Pascual, M. R. (2004). Traversing disparate cultures in a transnational world. In A. González, M. Houston, & V. Chen (Eds.), *Our voices: Essays on culture, ethnicity, and communication* (4th ed.) (pp. 288–297). Roxbury.

Rowe, W., & Schelling, V. (1991). *Memory and modernity: Popular culture in Latin America*. Verso.

Roy, C. (2005). *Traditional festivals: A multicultural encyclopedia*. ABC-CLIO, Inc.

Sarup, M. (1996). *Identity, culture and the postmodern world*. University of Georgia Press.

See, S. B. O. (2015, September 17). Playing the Mooncake Festival's centuries-old dice game. *GMA News Online*. https://www.gmanetwork.com/news/lifestyle/artandculture/537272/playing-the-mooncake-festival-s-centuries-old-dice-game/story/

Shi, Y. (2005). Identity construction of the Chinese diaspora, ethnic media use, community formation, and the possibility of social activism. *Continuum: Journal of Media & Cultural Studies, 19*(1), 55–72. https://doi.org/10.1080/1030431052000336298

Thompson, R. M. (2003). *Filipino English and Taglish: Language switching from multiple perspectives*. John Benjamins.

Wenjing, X. (2005). Virtual space, real identity: Exploring cultural identity of Chinese diaspora in virtual community. *Telematics & Informatics, 22*(4), 395–404. https://doi.org/10.1016/j.tele.2004.11.006

Yep, G. A. (2002). My three cultures: Navigating the multicultural identity landscape. In J. Martin, T. Nakayama, & L. Flores (Eds.), *Readings in intercultural communication: Experiences and contexts* (2nd ed., pp. 60–66). McGraw-Hill.

GENERATIONAL TSINA/OYS: (AUTO)ETHNOGRAPHIC REFLECTIONS AND FUTURE DIRECTIONS

January 15, 2018. My cell phone alerts me with a new text message at 6:45 a.m. A van driver is waiting outside my house to take me and my family to the Los Angeles International Airport (LAX). As I gather my things, I have realized it has been about seven years since the last time I traveled to Manila. However, this trip is special because, along with my spouse, my father, son, and I—three generations of Tsinoys—are going to Manila together. My father, who has not gone back to Manila since we immigrated to the United States 25 years earlier, is particularly looking forward to this trip. With all luggage stowed away in the van, we head to LAX. We arrive at the Bradley International Terminal an hour later. Checking in at the airline counter desk, all four of us receive our boarding passes with a connecting flight to Hong Kong before landing in Manila.

Arriving in Manila at 10:30 p.m. local time, we exit the gate and head to the baggage claim area to pick up our luggage. Upon collecting our belongings after several rounds of luggage circling around the carousel, we walk to the curbside outside the terminal waiting for my aunt. About half an hour later, my aunt approaches us while calling my name. Considering how congested the airport terminal is even late at night, we follow her pointing to where the van is located. Clearly not parked properly, we hurry along to toss all the luggage in the back of the van and take our seats immediately. Driving through the city of Manila is reminiscent of my initial trip here about seven years ago, minus the Christmas decorations and lights blanketing the city. There is no question that my aunt is excited to see us. My father, who sits right beside my aunt, converses with her about how the city has changed since the last time he was here. As the van gets closer to my grandmother and aunt's apartment, my aunt confirms with us that my father will be sleeping in their apartment, while my spouse, son, and I will be staying at a nearby hotel.

In the heart of the Chinatown neighborhood in Binondo, we arrive at Ramada Manila Central, which is only a couple of blocks from my aunt and grandmother's apartment. Located on Ongpin Street, the hotel's appeal to the ethnic Chinese community is hard to miss for its bold red lettering identifying the hotel by name and red lanterns hanging in front of the building. My aunt accompanies me and my family to the hotel to ensure that we can check-in successfully. With the check-in process complete, my aunt reminds me to drop by the apartment in the morning.

January 17, 2018. It is a new day in Manila, and the time zone difference has become apparent for my lack of sleep. Coming down to the front steps of the hotel to go to my aunt and grandmother's apartment reminds me I am here as a visitor. However, given that I was born and raised in Manila, I also feel like I have returned home. As planned, my spouse, my son, and I make our trek to my aunt and grandmother's apartment. Within a five-minute walk, we arrive at our destination. I see the familiar dining room immediately upon entering the apartment's front door where my grandmother, aunt, and father have been waiting for our arrival. Greeting and kissing my grandmother, she meets my spouse and son for the first time. She smiles and compliments them simultaneously. We all sit down quickly at the table for lunch. Recalling the last time I visited about seven years ago, my grandmother is happy that I came back once again with my family.

Now at 102, my grandmother is still as talkative as I have always known her. However, one distinct difference from the last time I saw her is her lack of mobility. As one would probably expect for her age, she needs assistance to stand up and move about the apartment. I also learned she does not go out as much anymore. Despite these limitations, she can maintain lengthy conversations with anyone. With her usual directness, she instructs everyone to eat as much as possible. As we are all munching all the dishes before us, my grandmother notices that her great-grandson is having a difficult time eating seemingly foreign foods. Wanting to communicate with her great-grandson, my grandmother asks us if he could speak Hokkien. My father responds immediately, "*Bô la. Eng-bûn lang*" ["No, English only"]. My aunt offers her perspective: "*Ya tse-toa na*" ["It's such a waste"]. Without feeling offended, my aunt's comment about my son's inability to speak Hokkien or Chinese in general makes me wonder, though, about the challenges and possibilities ahead for future generations of Tsina/oys.

The (in)ability to communicate in Hokkien continues to be one of the many challenges facing Tsina/oys today. In fact, many young Tsina/oys have lost the ability to speak, read, and write in Chinese (See, 1997). Through ethnographic interviews conducted in 2010 and 2011 and autoethnographic reflections, I examine in this concluding chapter how Tsina/oyness could change and evolve in Manila and beyond. First, I discuss how generational differences contribute to Tsina/oy participants' perception of what it means to be "Tsina/oy." I continue with how participants (re)defined Tsina/oyness to legitimize its locality in the Philippines. Finally, I close with what I have learned about (trans)national Tsina/oy identity.

Generational Constructions and Perceptions of Tsina/oy Identity

Similar to my aunt, many Tsina/oys, especially from the baby boomer generation, have expressed great concern about the potential loss of younger Tsina/oys' Chinese culture. One of my Tsina/oy participants, Dino, confirmed the same concern: "Well, uh, in my [baby boomer] generation, we feel more like, eh, more on Chinese because we're the second generation, but to my children I think they're more Filipino." Due to generational differences, Tsina/oy participants conveyed that family upbringing, assimilation, and institutional practices have contributed to the changing nature of Tsina/oy identity. Anson and Lydia gave their perspective as second-generation Tsina/oys on how family upbringing plays a major role in shaping Tsina/oy identity:

ANSON: I'm feeling if parents start to talk in Tagalog and English, you're sending already a message *parang ganon* [like that]. Some of my friends, who are Chinese, they at least speak Chinese [Hokkien] at home with their parents. That's why they're more Chinese. They have a lot of Chinese culture.

LYDIA: Those people whose parents are half Chinese, half Filipino, and they're not... they [parents] don't send them [children] to Chinese school...they [children] don't study in Chinese school, they don't mingle with the Chinese, so they think they are Filipino—more Filipino than they're Chinese.

Anson and Lydia both resonated with baby boomer Tsina/oys in part because traditional Chinese values, traditions, and practices have been embedded as part of their daily lives. Third- and fourth-generation Tsina/oys, on the other hand, tend to be exposed to both cultures, but perhaps more so to local Filipina/o cultural traditions and practices in some Tsina/oy families. Anson and Lydia also argued that parents play a major role in shaping their children's Tsina/oy identity. For instance, Anson noted parents' initiative to teach their child(ren) how to speak Hokkien at home could very well be a factor in maintaining their Chinese culture. In my case, while growing up in the Philippines, my parents communicated with me and my siblings primarily in Hokkien to embody our Chineseness. I believe that my ability to speak Hokkien has strengthened my identification with Tsinoy identity. Lydia went further by stating that some Tsina/oy parents do not send their child(ren) to Tsina/oy schools, which could have a tremendous impact on their Chinese identity. Although every Tsina/oy family has different circumstances, attending Tsina/oy school as a child benefited me greatly. Because of my primary education experience, I was exposed to both Chinese and Filipina/o cultural instruction that contributed to my academic and social awareness of Tsinoy identity.

Generational differences in family upbringing can also be understood through the embodiment of Chinese and Filipina/o traditions. Joy and Rachel shared their own perspectives:

JOY: Come to think of it, because our parents still follow the traditional way—the traditional Chinese things—but right now there are families that, you know, that totally don't follow the Chinese traditions so I think it [Tsina/oy identity] continues to evolve...I think people are starting to think about things, like logical things, like what will or what not to follow, so it [Tsina/oy] will change. It [Tsina/oy] will continue to change.

RACHEL: I'd say it [Tsina/oy] will continue to change eventually cos for my grandparents back then when they say "Tsinoy," it's a totally different meaning versus now. How I see it is like this: As much as possible, I want to have passed down my [Chinese] traditions to my kids, but then the traditions I learn or I truly believe in are probably 40% of authentic, original traditions, but by the time it gets to my grandkids and the kids afterwards it will become like 10% of that, really depends on how kids or I follow the traditions.

Contrary to the past when older Tsina/oys prioritized their Chinese over Filipina/o identity, new generations of Tsina/oys are likely to perform their hybridity as Chinese and Filipina/o based on changing times and environments. Both Joy and Rachel acknowledged that previous Tsina/oy generations have historically maintained Chinese traditions to perform their Chineseness as ethnic minorities in the Philippines. It is not unusual for hybrids in (trans)national spaces to engage in and maintain cultural traditions and practices. For example, Lum (2006) recounts the challenges of introducing and maintaining Chinese traditions and practices to his Chinese American children. Lum talks about the difficulty of celebrating Lunar New Year when it is not a public holiday in the United States, which restricts celebrating the holiday's cultural significance through food and other rituals at home. Like Lum's experience, the emergence of new generations of Tsina/oys has resulted in the alteration of Chinese traditions that reflect Tsina/oys who have adopted Filipina/o traditions and social practices. In fact, because of Spanish and U.S. colonization, Tsina/oys have been engaging in hybridized traditions and practices that represent both aspects of Chinese and Filipina/o cultures (See, 2004). As Joy articulated, many Tsina/oys engage in Chinese traditions that are "logical" to their current lifestyle and applicable to their cultural identification as Chinese and Filipina/o in the Philippines. It was not unusual, for instance, for my family and I to celebrate Lunar New Year by integrating Tsina/oy foods, such as *pansit* (noodles), *lumpia* (spring roll), and *tikoy* (glutinous rice cake). As Tsina/oys in the Philippines, my family and I celebrated Lunar New Year festivities at home that reflected our Chinese and Filipina/o cultures through food.

Assimilationist strategies among younger Tsina/oys are another contributing factor that make it difficult for them to maintain their Chineseness. Some Tsina/oys engage in assimilationist performances to combat the historical construction of Tsina/oys as foreign Others (Chu, 2021). More specifically, Lulu, Ethel, and Rachel talked about how they or other Tsina/oys they know have faced ethnic stereotypes that could be subjected to masking their Chinese identity:

LULU: When I was a teenager in school, we cannot be equal [to Filipina/os for] speaking Chinese because Filipinos would be "Ching-a Chong-o." They will laugh at you, not even behind your back like "Ha-ha-ha," and then they will say "Ching-a Chong-o." They will imitate how you speak.

ETHEL: I, myself, studied in Philippine school and we're about two or three Chinese talking [in] Chinese and sometimes Filipinos would "Ching Chong," something like that. *Parang pinag pa tawaran ka* [Like they are laughing at you], so sometimes you pretend to not talk [in Chinese] anymore...because of your own personal safety.

RACHEL: I had a classmate like that, too. Um, he's actually Chinese, but his last name, um, apparently, sounds very Filipino so he tries to get away with that [not identifying as Chinese] when people ask him. Cos he knows Chinese, he understands it. It's just that when people try to talk to him, he pretends he doesn't [know Chinese]. I don't know if he's ashamed or just doesn't want to be associated [with being Chinese] because people have—society here in the Philippines—tend to have a general idea that Chinese or Tsinoy are a bit snobbish, rich, stingy. They're pretty much rich.

Many Tsina/oys have been accustomed to hearing, while in the presence of some Filipina/os, anti-Chinese remarks like "Ching Chong" or something similar. Furthermore, some Tsina/oys have chosen not to disclose their Chinese identity for fear of mockery. Consequently, some Tsina/oys may assimilate to mainstream Filipina/o culture by delegitimizing their Chinese identity. Like other multicultural individuals, Tsina/oys perform the "dialectical tension of cultural assimilation and cultural preservation" as they negotiate "intercultural differences" in mainstream society (Young, 2009, p. 155). Performing in-betweenness, Tsina/oys assert their Filipina/o identity by speaking Tagalog in the company of other Filipina/os while engaging in Chinese cultural and linguistic practices at home and in the Tsina/oy community.

In addition to family upbringing and assimilation, the changing dynamics of Tsina/oy identity can be attributed to institutional practices in the Philippines. Esmeralda gave an example of how media and schooling in the Philippines have had great effects on Tsina/oy identity:

Back in the day, we had Chinese programs on TV, and we watched Chinese movies subtitled [and] it's all in Mandarin. Nowadays, even Chinese programs, they have translations; they [are] dubbed with Filipino words. And then the school, the Chinese subjects *na* minus *na* [have been eliminated]. *Gusto nila mag oriented sa* Filipino [Legislators want the Chinese to be oriented with Filipino culture]. As a result, even when teaching Mandarin, it's more like just reading in Chinese but not speaking it.

Besides schools, institutions like the media serve as public pedagogies that can have tremendous impact on cultural identity (Sandlin et al., 2010). Mediated texts, such as television programs, serve as public pedagogies due to their influential power to educate the audience on "the developments of identities and social formations" (p. 1). Focusing on Chinese programming in the Philippines, Esmeralda claimed it has changed over the years with current dubbing of the actors' voices with "Filipino words," which restricts the ability for Tsina/oys to hear, understand, and learn Mandarin. Esmeralda also critiqued restrictions imposed on how Chinese subjects are taught in Tsina/oy schools as an effort to assimilate Tsina/oys into Philippine society. In fact, as part of the Filipinization policy instituted in the 1935, 1973, and 1987 Constitutions of the Philippines,

Tsina/oy schools have been required to provide Tagalog language and Filipina/o citizenship instruction (Almonte-Acosta, 2012). Even though Chinese subjects are taught in schools, some Tsina/oys like Esmeralda thought that Chinese language instruction is treated as supplementary education, which limits its full potential to teach Tsina/oys how to speak Hokkien and Mandarin fluently.

As part of the institutional practice of preserving Chinese identity, Wayne called for local Tsina/oy leaders and businesses to take it upon themselves to teach younger Tsina/oy generations the importance of maintaining their Chineseness. He said, "The challenge for Chinese business and cultural leaders is to find a way to preserve the Chinese culture." As "each generation progresses," Wayne noted that Tsina/oys "naturally learn" about Filipina/o culture so it is crucial to teach younger Tsina/oys about their Chinese culture. There is no doubt that the challenges for Tsina/oys to maintain their Chinese culture are ongoing; however, the recent arrival of Chinese migrants has also become a concern for Tsina/oys to be protective of their local Chinese status in the Philippines.

"Genuine *Intsik*": Distinguishing Tsina/oy Identity

January 18, 2018. As I learn more about the Chinese migrants in Manila, my aunt informs me that many of them have established businesses locally. Less than half a mile from my grandmother and aunt's apartment, my spouse, son, and I take a leisurely walk to the 168 Shopping Mall (also known as "168" for short). Upon arrival, we see a multi-story bright blue building that is clearly marked with "168 Shopping Mall." In front and around the mall, the street is crowded with local vendors selling foods, drinks, and other items to attract shoppers entering and leaving the mall. Unlike a typical mall that carries domestic and imported brands, 168 is what locals call a *"tiangge,"* a market that is set up with stalls that sell bargain-priced clothes, shoes, toys, home goods, accessories, and other everyday items.

The air-conditioned building is filled with countless stalls. The walking paths are narrow, making them difficult to get through other people walking in both directions. My son spots a digital watch that transforms into a robot, so we stop at the stall that sells the item. Talking to the Filipina salesperson, I try to haggle the price with her in Tagalog. The Chinese owner, however, interjects in Tagalog that 250 pesos (about $5) is the lowest price he can offer. Satisfied with the price, I buy the watch. Given that this is my first time at 168,

I am surprised to find out that the vendors occupying these storefronts are predominantly recent Chinese migrants from mainland China. In fact, "almost 90%" of business stalls in shopping malls in the Manila area are "owned or rented by Chinese migrants" (Dai, 2017, p. 178).

Despite China's rise in economic power, recent Chinese migrants have come to the Philippines because of insufficient economic opportunities in China's villages and rural areas (Dai, 2017). Dai further notes that investment and employment-based immigration became an impetus for a lot of Chinese to immigrate to the Philippines. For example, after becoming law in 2009, the Special Visa for Employment Generation "is issued to qualified non-immigrant foreigners who agree to employ at least ten Filipinos in a lawful and sustainable enterprise, trade or industry" (p. 172). Alternatively, an immigrant visa is also issued to the Chinese who marry Filipina/o citizens. Despite these visa incentives, the reality is many Chinese migrants have overstayed on tourist or business visa and become undocumented over time.

The Philippines is an attractive place for Chinese migrants to start a business due to the following factors: low cost to operate a business, strong Filipina/o purchasing power, lack of competition commercially, established family and coethnic networks, and lack of immigration law enforcement (Dai, 2017). Of all places in the Philippines, Manila's Chinatown in Binondo "acts as a magnet for new Chinese migrants and serves their daily and business needs" (p. 177). Built in 1594, Binondo still remains one of the biggest and oldest Chinatowns in the world today (Tan, 2013). Like many Tsina/oys, most recent Chinese migrants are from the Fujian province and speak Hokkien, making Binondo an ideal transitional home for them. Even though they lack proficiency in Tagalog and English, Chinese migrants are still able to thrive in Binondo because of social and cultural networks that are afforded to them.

With the Manila area continues to serve as a new home for Chinese migrants, shopping malls like 168 have exploded in Binondo and surrounding vicinities in Quezon City and Greenhills since the mid-1990s because of local demand for affordable goods (Dai, 2017). Due to rapid surge of Chinese migrants and their business ventures, concerns among Tsina/oys are growing. As Dai (2017) reports, "The arrival of new immigrants can lead to competition and conflicts with Chinese Filipinos. The latter complain that Chinese migrants violate business rules and local laws in order to make quick money" (p. 182). Because there have been cases of new Chinese migrants' involvement with "illegal activities," Tsina/oys worry such behaviors could "hurt both local society and the interests of the newcomers themselves" (p. 182).

Given the recent wave of Chinese migration to the Philippines, especially in the Manila area, it is worth exploring how it has shaped Tsina/oy identity. Because of the negative reputation that Chinese migrants often get, many Tsina/oys try to distinguish themselves by using "Genuine *Intsik*" or G.I. in reference to Chinese migrants or Chinese individuals who were born and/or raised in China. According to Chu (2021), *intsik* is "a vernacular term [that Filipina/os use] to refer to the Chinese" (p. 3). More specifically, many publications and societal representations of the Chinese who immigrated to the Philippines were often called "*intsik*" and described as dirty and uncivilized in Spanish literature and other writings in the late 1800s (Chu, 2021). In particular, Hau (2000) notes that the derogatory phrase "*intsik viejo, tulo laway*" ["Old Chinese drooling"] was popularized during the U.S. colonization period (p. 301). Despite its "assumed negative connotations," "*intsik*" is still a common term used today that is also being reclaimed by some Chinese Filipina/os themselves (Chu, 2021, p. 3).

Since G.I. refers to Chinese individuals from China, Tsina/oys often consider G.I.s as "authentic" or "traditional" Chinese because of their geographical ties to mainland China and embodiment of traditional Chinese values and cultural practices. Joy described the following traits for a G.I.:

> Here in the Philippines, when you say authentic or genuine Chinese, like FOB or Fresh off the Boat kind of thing. They call it "Genuine *Intsik*," [a] completely racist term, and those are the ones "TDK" (*tai-diok-ka*) from mainland China. My point of view is that there's such a thing as authentic Chinese, but I think I call it "traditional Chinese" rather than "authentic Chinese." Yeah, that's what I think. There are people who are traditional Chinese and also the, you know, westernized Chinese people who follow different types of traditions. I'm tainted [laughs]. I'm not the traditional-type Chinese person, no. I think I'm not. I have a huge percentage of Chinese traditions I still follow, but not all—not really the by-the-book Chinese—you know, yeah, no, I don't think so.

Joy described what "Genuine *Intsik*" (G.I.) means, which is also commonly known as "*tai-diok-ka*" (TDK), a Hokkien term used for mainland Chinese people (Chu, 2021). Joy made a connection between "Genuine *Intsik*" and "*tai-diok-ka*," which is important to point out because the word "genuine" is used to authenticate one's Chinese identity that is bound by traditions and geography (mainland China). Both Christian and Tina also confirmed Joy's understanding of G.I. as someone from mainland China originally:

CHRISTIAN: *Góa boeh kam-kak góa ka lan-nang tē. Góa boeh kam-kak G.I. eh. Hwaí lan-nang tē góa bô lō. Góa tē-dī tāi, so góa pá mì lo. Góa dī-chap it hòe tsa lâi chia* [I don't feel I'm Chinese. I don't feel G.I. I don't have those Chinese ways. Those who came from China are Chinese. I'm second-generation Chinese in the Philippines, so I'm different from those in China. I came to the Philippines when I was 21 years old].

TINA: I don't know if you call it authentic, *pero* [but] we call here G.I.—Genuine *Intsik*! [Laughs]. I think *yung parang* [those may be] very Chinese guy *talaga na ano yan* [really have] super Chinese thinking, yes, *oo* [yes]. In terms of looks, in terms of, um, what do you call it, behaviors, *ano ba* [what is it]? Of course, yes. Yeah, yeah. *Ako danito* [I'm like this], I'm more Filipino actually. I was born here, I was raised here, but values—Chinese—like hard working, my parents are businessmen—those are Chinese. You said *kanina yung mga* values [You said earlier about values], traditions and what I practice, something like that, birthdays *ganon* [like that], *oo* [yes].

Based on Christian and Tina's responses, "Genuine *Intsik*" (G.I.) is a term that is used to define Chinese people from China who can be legitimized as "authentic Chinese." As a second-generation Chinese in the Philippines, Christian did not feel he can claim Chinese authenticity; his experiences have been "different" from those in China. Like Christian, Tina also considered those from China as G.I. In addition, she explained that G.I.s exhibit specific "Chinese" behaviors, values, and traditions. By contrast, Tina made it clear that she is "more Filipino" since she was born and raised in the Philippines. As Appadurai (1996) puts it, transnational movements establish hybrid collectivity among people who live in diaspora. As recent generations of Chinese Filipina/os, (trans)national Tsina/oys have established collective Chinese and Filipina/o identities. As a result, many Tsina/oys distinguish themselves from G.I.s due to their bicultural identities and values.

The presence of G.I.s, especially recent Chinese migrants, will continue to affect local Tsina/oys culturally. They have influenced Tsina/oys to reconsider what it means to be "Chinese" and "Tsina/oy." Dan and Tanya gave their own insights on Chinese migrants' impact on Tsina/oys:

DAN: I think it [the meaning of Tsina/oy] will continue to change...As for now, there's a significant portion [of Tsina/oys] that's [practicing] Filipino [traditions], but with all the influx of the new Chinese [migrant] people here there's a certain shift towards to a more [appreciation of] Chinese side again. It's going to go back to another [Chinese] side.

TANYA: I guess, uh, we're hoping that maybe in the future we don't need this special labeling [Tsina/oy], but we cannot disregard that, especially with the new immigrants coming in. The legal new immigrants—we welcome them; they have done a lot for us, but the problem is with the illegal immigrants that have committed a lot of crimes here, and the media's fondness for racial labeling that everybody is Chinese is what's this really making us assert the word "Tsinoy" even more, but we hope in the future generation there's no need for that distinction.

Based on Dan and Tanya's responses, they cited recent Chinese migration's influence on Tsina/oy identity. With newer generations of Tsina/oys who are becoming less inclined to practice their Chinese culture, Dan indicated the presence of recent Chinese migrants could reignite the Chinese pride among Tsina/oys. By contrast, Tanya argued "illegal" Chinese migrants have fueled many Chinese in the Philippines to identify as "Tsina/oys." It is important to note that Tanya distinguished Chinese migrants from Tsina/oys based on their immigration status (legal or otherwise). Therefore, making such a distinction is to legitimize Tsina/oys' localized bodies in the Philippines.

Despite the negative perception of recent Chinese migrants, Tsina/oy participants seemed to credit China's status as a global economic power in shaping the meaning of Tsina/oy identity. The dialectic between the negative perception of Chinese migration to the Philippines and China's rise economically has contributed to Tsina/oys' performance of "politics of location" (Hall, 1996, p. 2). As a result, many Tsina/oys have negotiated their hybridity by distancing themselves from Chinese migrants while embracing their Chinese culture more than before. For instance, many Tsina/oys talked about taking steps to learn how to speak Mandarin fluently. A few Tsina/oy participants offered their thoughts:

RITA: But, uh, especially nowadays, they [younger Tsina/oys] started to recognize themselves as Tsinoy because of, um, the China boom.

DENISA: I think it [the meaning of Tsina/oy] will continue to change. It all depends on China [laughs]. Maybe if China will continue to become one of the great nations, maybe the Tsinoys will become more Chinese. Yes, more Chinese because right now there are more Tsinoys wanting to speak Mandarin. They want more of China, and then the parents here...many of them are sending their children to Beijing to study the Chinese language.

LULU: I think maybe in a few years' time when the next decade maybe when China starts to be more and more powerful whether military-wise or economic-wise the Tsinoys here will start, uh, like wanting more to learn the Chinese language.

WAYNE: So, as China becomes better, many Chinese in the Philippines would want to learn Chinese and that will change the definition of Tsinoy. A lot of the Chinese Filipinos today will do international business in China that will force

[them] to speak Mandarin. China as an economic miracle will change the definition that will revitalize the Chinese culture in some sense [but] not entirely.

From their experiences and interactions with other Tsina/oys, Rita, Denisa, Lulu, and Wayne had no reservations in believing that China's status as an economic superpower has already impacted Tsina/oyness in some way. While it has been difficult for younger Tsina/oys to maintain Chinese cultural traditions and practices, Rita, Denisa, Lulu, and Wayne claimed that China's powerful image could reignite younger Tsina/oys' interest in their Chinese identity. Entering the global marketplace, some Tsina/oy participants talked about the need for Tsina/oys to learn how to speak Mandarin fluently to gain professional opportunities in China and abroad. China's meteoric rise in the world stage has prompted Tsina/oys to reconsider the significance of their Chineseness that could impact their identity development for years to come.

(Re)Discovering (Trans)national Tsina/oyness

January 21, 2018. Thinking about the future of Tsina/oy identity, I look at my multigenerational Tsina/oy family members eating dinner with me at a buffet restaurant. Sitting at a long mahogany table with loved ones resembles a mini-family reunion. The seating arrangement is not planned, but we seem to find our appropriate seats. My spouse, son, and I sit adjacent to my cousins, while my father sits next to his sister and brother. After gathering our foods and setting them on the table, my cousin, the eldest daughter of my uncle, expresses how ecstatic she is to see us. I first met my cousin when she and her parents used to live in a suburban area of Los Angeles in 1992. Reflecting back a couple of decades ago, I ask her if she could recall the time when my family and I came to Los Angeles as tourists. With a big smile, she remembers our visit and her childhood in the United States vividly. As a millennial Tsinay who has a Chinese Filipino father and Taiwanese mother, she is multilingual with fluency in Hokkien, Mandarin, Tagalog, and English. As we continue our conversation, my cousin asks about my son's age and if he goes to school. At five years old, my son, who is in kindergarten, does not have a full grasp of being in Manila except for a family trip. While responding to my cousin's queries, I can't help but to stare at my son sitting among us as a member of our Tsina/oy family.

Watching the mini-family reunion take place is bittersweet. After all, enjoying a feast with my extended family tonight is also a reminder that my journey here in Manila is about to end. My third visit to Manila is a much different experience from my previous trips because I traveled with my spouse, son, and father. In many ways, it is special to have three generations of my immediate family reuniting with other family members. Above all, my father's reunion with his loved ones has been remarkable. Seeing my father's joy while visiting Manila is so much more to going back home; it is also about (re)discovering our Tsinoyness through my father's eyes.

January 23, 2018. Two days after the buffet dinner, it is time for my spouse, son, father, and I to depart Manila for Los Angeles. There is no certainty of when any of us will be visiting Manila again. As I take out my passport to show the airline representative, I am reminded that I am now a Tsinoy American. Having traveled to the Philippines for three times now, I have learned a lot about the (trans)national nature of Tsina/oy identity that can be performed within and beyond the national constraints of the Philippines as a nation-state.

Engaging in critical ethnographic interviews, autoethnography, and cyberethnography provided me opportunities to analyze Tsina/oyness as (trans)national and intersectional identities in both physical and online spaces. Following Alexander's (1999) influential work, utilizing a multimethodological approach to ethnography helped articulate and reflect diverse storied lives of (trans)national Tsina/oys. Conducting critical ethnographic interviews in the Philippines allowed me to examine Tsina/oy voices that offered different perspectives on what it means to be "Tsina/oy." Integrating Critical Intercultural Performance (CIP) as a framework to analyze Tsina/oy experiences communicated the significance of combining critical intercultural communication and performance studies to acknowledge the performative and fluid nature of identities. In addition, emphasizing intersectionality and reflexivity, I utilized CIP to highlight my (trans)national hybrid researcher positionality and subjectivity to learn with and from multilingual participants about their embodiments of ethnic, national, and class identities. Some Tsina/oy participants, especially those from the baby boomer generation, stated they tend to prioritize their Chineseness through social and cultural practices. On the other hand, younger generations of Tsina/oys continue to recognize their Chineseness while performing their Filipina/o identity. Regardless of generational differences, some Tsina/oys engage in assimilationist strategies to fit into mainstream Philippine society.

I also used critical autoethnography to reflect on my Tsinoyness as a *balikbayan* or cultural returnee. Critiquing the cultural reentry literature, which tends to reinforce the home/host binary, I argued the significance of recognizing that short-term reentries do occur. With my *balikbayan* identity, I consider myself as a (trans)national Tsinoy American who calls Los Angeles (current place of residence) and Manila (birthplace) home. As economic and political conditions continue to redefine borders, we must also think of cultural identities beyond the nation-state standpoint (Anthias, 2001; Appadurai, 1996). To this end, I believe that Tsina/oys who live, work, or study in between and beyond national borders can embody their Tsina/oy identity (trans)nationally.

As someone who recently became a U.S. citizen in 2016, I reflected autoethnographically on what it was like to claim and lose a national identity as part of the naturalization process. Even though it was a joyous occasion to become a U.S. citizen, participating in the Oath of Allegiance ceremony proved to be challenging emotionally. I had difficulty wrapping my head around the reality of gaining a new nationality as a U.S. American while simultaneously losing my Filipino citizenship, which confirmed the Philippines as home—a place to reminisce my Tsinoy childhood. As Cohen (1997) remarks, it is not unusual for (trans)national hybrids to feel the tension of remaining loyal to both the homeland and where one decides to live permanently. While I no longer have my Filipino citizenship, my Filipino identity is always a part of my Tsinoyness no matter where I am. After all, multicultural identities are about the collective experience that shapes one's self-concept in the process (Cupach & Imahori, 1993; Yep, 2002).

Beyond the physical borders of nation-states, (trans)national Tsina/oys can also perform their hybridity in cyberspace. Discovering Tsinoy.com gave me a chance to engage in cyberethnography to learn about Tsina/oys around the world who used online discussion forums to communicate their (trans)national Tsina/oy identity, practices, and traditions. I found it striking that Tsinoy.com participants had a variety of perspectives on how their Tsina/oyness could be reconstructed culturally across borders. Through their online posts, I gained a lot of insight about a Tsina/oy community that blurred virtual and physical worlds. I agree with Gajjala (2004) that online members can (re)present their lives online, and Tsinoy.com mirrored the realities of Tsina/oys where they communicated Chinese and Filipina/o identities from wherever they were located.

More importantly, Tsinoy.com made it possible for Tsina/oys to have a voice—a voice that otherwise would have been dismissed for the mere fact they were online. Like other Tsina/oys, Tsinoy.com members dealt with multiple tensions by resisting fixed and stable traditions and practices (Gómez-Peña,

1996) and pushing discourses of Tsina/oyness beyond its construction simply as Chinese and Filipina/o identities in the Philippines. Regardless of location (countries, cultural borders, or online), Tsinoy.com communicated that Tsina/oys are (trans)national for their diverse historicities and navigating in-between cultural spaces.

January 23, 2018. Like Tsinoy.com members, my (trans)national body is always moving in-between spaces. After almost a day of traveling between continents, my spouse, son, father, and I have returned home to Los Angeles. Upon arriving at the Los Angeles International Airport, we all follow our way through customs. Before presenting our documents to the USCIS official, we must scan our passports by using the touch screen monitor. The process is straightforward by taking a quick photo, answering a few questions, and scanning the passport from the monitor. However, since my father is not a U.S. citizen, he must also scan and answer questions related to his permanent residency card. Noticing this extra step for my father's arrival process, I inquire if he ever considered applying for U.S. citizenship. While waiting in line at the airport, he responds in Hokkien without hesitation: "*Bô tèng-iōng. Góa lāu lo!*" ["It's no use. I'm already old!"]. For as long as I can remember, getting a permanent residency in the United States was my father's goal as an immigrant. The "green card" was his dream for his family to provide some stability in the future. He achieved his goal and is content with what the permanent residency can offer him legally. For whatever reason, he never insisted on becoming a U.S. citizen. Perhaps, for my father, he did not need to subscribe to the white "American Dream" of U.S. citizenship; he only needed to secure a stable future for his family to make it possible for us to pursue our own dreams.

Finally arriving home past 10 p.m., we are all exhausted from our trip. Our bodies tell us to go to bed instantly. The next morning, I drive my father back to my parents' house, which is an hour away from where I live. While driving, I strike up a conversation with my father to see if he slept well. He confirms that he had a good night's sleep. He proceeds to tell me that he was glad that I brought him with my family to visit my grandmother, aunt, and other family members in Manila. It was a long-awaited and memorable reunion for him. I could tell he was overjoyed for having the opportunity to see his family. It took my father 25 years to go back home, and it meant a lot to him, especially not knowing if he will have another opportunity anytime soon. No matter what happens in the future, our trip to Manila was life-changing for (re)discovering ourselves as (trans)national Tsinoys.

References

Alexander, B. K. (1999). Performing culture in the classroom: An instructional (auto)ethnography. *Text and Performance Quarterly, 19*(4), 307–331. https://doi.org/10.1080/10462939909366272

Almonte-Acosta, S. A. (2012). Pedagogical approaches to citizenship education in the varied contexts of secondary schools in the Philippines. In K. J. Kennedy, W. O. Lee, & D. L. Grossman (Eds.), *Citizenship pedagogies in Asia and the Pacific* (pp. 175–201). Springer Science & Business Media.

Anthias, F. (2001). New hybridities, old concepts: The limits of "culture." *Ethnic and Racial Studies, 24*(4), 619–641. https://doi.org/10.1080/01419870120049815

Appadurai, A. (1996). *Modernity at large: Cultural dimensions of globalization*. University of Minnesota Press.

Chu, R. T. (2021). From "Sangley" to "Chinaman", "Chinese mestizo" to "Tsinoy": Unpacking "Chinese" identities in the Philippines at the turn of the Twentieth-Century. *Asian Ethnicity*, 1–31. https://doi.org/10.1080/14631369.2021.1941755

Cohen, R. (1997). *Global diasporas: An introduction*. UCL Press.

Cupach, W. R., & Imahori, T. T. (1993). Identity management theory: Communication competence in intercultural episodes and relationships. In R. L. Wiseman & J. Koester (Eds.), *Intercultural communication competence* (pp. 112–131). SAGE.

Dai, F. (2017). Chinese immigration to the Philippines since the late 1970s. In M. Zhou (Ed.), *Contemporary Chinese diasporas* (pp. 167–186). Palgrave Macmillan. https://doi.org/10.1007/978-981-10-5595-9_8

Gajjala, R. (2004). *Cyber selves: Feminist ethnographies of South Asian women*. AltaMira Press.

Gómez-Peña, G. (1996). *The new world border: Prophesies, poems and loqueras for the end of the century*. City Lights.

Hall, S. (1996). Introduction: Who needs "identity"? In S. Hall & P. du Gay (Eds.), *Questions of cultural identity* (pp. 1–17). SAGE.

Hau, C. S. (2000). *Intsik: An anthology of Chinese-Filipino writing*. Anvil.

Lum, C. M. K. (2006). Communicating Chinese heritage in America: A study of bicultural education across generations. In W. Leeds-Hurwitz (Ed.), *From generation to generation: Maintaining cultural identity over time* (pp. 75–98). Hampton Press.

Sandlin, J. A., Schultz, B. D., & Burdick, J. (2010). Understanding, mapping, and exploring the terrain of public pedagogy. In J. A. Sandlin, B. D. Shultz, & J. Burdick (Eds.), *Handbook of public pedagogy: Education and learning beyond schooling* (pp. 1–6). Routledge.

See, T. A. (1997). *Chinese in the Philippines: Problems & perspectives* (Vol. 1). Kaisa Para Sa Kaunlaran.

See, T. A. (2004). *Chinese in the Philippines: Problems & perspectives* (Vol. 3). Kaisa Para Sa Kaunlaran.

Tan, C. (2013). Chinatowns: A reflection. In B. P. Wong & C. Tan (Eds.), *Chinatowns around the world: Gilded ghetto, ethnopolis, and cultural diaspora* (pp. 263–284). Brill.

Yep, G. A. (2002). My three cultures: Navigating the multicultural identity landscape. In J. N. Martin, L. A. Flores, & T. K. Nakayama (Eds.), *Readings in intercultural communication: Experiences and contexts* (2nd ed., pp. 60–66). McGraw-Hill.

Young, S. L. (2009). Half and half: An (auto)ethnography of hybrid identities in a Korean American mother-daughter relationship. *Journal of International and Intercultural Communication, 2*(2), 139–167. https://doi.org/10.1080/17513050902759512

INDEX

A

acculturation 80
Adams, T. E. 34, 35
Adler, N. J. 77
Alcoff, L. M. 32
Alexander, B. K. 8, 9, 10, 11, 13, 14, 15, 27, 31, 32, 33, 35, 36, 64, 123
Allen, C. 72
Almonte-Acosta, S. A. 117
Anderson, B. 7, 77
Anthias, F. 7, 8, 10, 11, 12, 63, 83, 93, 96, 124
Anzaldúa, G. 8, 10, 11, 14, 49, 63, 103, 104, 107
Aparicio, F. R. 8
Appadurai, A. 7, 10, 92, 104, 107, 120, 124
Appiah, K. A. 95
assimilation 50, 80, 113, 115–116
Atay, A. 35, 37
Atkinson, P. 27, 31
Augustin, L. 104
autoethnography
  as research 34–35
  critical approach to *see* critical autoethnography
  definition of 33–34
  historical background of 34–35
  intersectionality 35, 73
  other names for 35
  types of 35

B

baby boomers 54, 113–114, 123
Baig, N. 79, 82, 83, 84, 85
Bakhtin, M. M. 10, 49
balikbayan
  Balikbayan Program 76–77
  as cultural returnees 73, 75–77, 85–87, 123–124
  definition of 76–77
  OCWs (Overseas Contract Workers) 76
Banks, A. 33, 34
Banks, S. P. 33, 34
Bardhan, N. 7, 8

Barro, J. 72
Basch, L. 8, 92
Basu, A. 35
Bautista, M. L. S. 6
Bautista, R. 60
Baym, N. K. 38
Bell, D. 39
Bernal, M. E. 54
Berry, K. 35, 36
Besserer, F. 7, 8
Bhabha, H. 10, 11, 12, 49, 65, 95
Binondo *see* Chinatown
Black, J. S. 77
Blanc, C. S. 76, 108
Bochner, A. 34, 35
Bourdieu, P. 106
Boylorn, R. M. 32, 33, 35, 36
Brabant, S. 77
Brah, A. 8
Butler, J. 50

C

Calafell, B. M. 8, 10, 13, 14, 15, 16, 32, 35, 36, 49
Cariño, T. C. 5, 6, 59
Carless, D. 36
Carspecken, P. F. 28, 31
Catterall, M. 39
Certeau, M. de 14, 98–99
Chang, H. 33
Chang, Y. Y. 77–78, 80, 85
Chawla, D. 35, 106
Chen, Y.-W. 15–16
Cheng, H.-I. 8
Cherny, L. 38
China
 southern area of 3, 5
 economic power of 98, 118, 121–122
 economic opportunities in 3, 118
Chinatown
 Binondo 2, 4, 10, 26, 79, 112, 118
 businesses in 62, 118
 networks in 118
 transitional home for migrants 118
 Tsina/oys in 4, 118
Chinese Exclusion Act 4
Chinese in the Philippines
 anti-Chinese remarks 115–116
 Chinese businesses 57, 117–118
 Chinese Filipina/o identity 3, 6, 48–51, 54–56, 62–63, 80, 95, 103, 106, 119–120
 Chinese (im)migrants 4–6, 48, 54, 61–62, 117–121
 class identity 5, 57, 59–61, 66, 116
 discrimination against 4
 foods 7, 39, 99, 102, 115
 land ownership 4
 merchants 4
 naturalization of 5–6, 49, 52
 professional opportunities for 5, 49, 52, 122
 religious practices 4, 6
 schools 5, 54, 59, 99, 113–117
 stereotypes of 58–60
Chinese New Year *see* Lunar New Year
Chrifi Alaoui, F. Z. 14, 15
Chu, R. T. 4, 5, 62, 115, 119
Chua, A. 5, 57
Church, K. 35
Class
 positions of power 58
 rich/poor binary 57, 59
 stereotypes 58–60
Clifford, J. 7, 78, 79
Cohen, R. 124
Collier, M. J. 13, 94
Collins, P. H. 14
Conquergood, D. 14, 30, 31, 35
Córdoba, M. S. T. 8
Crenshaw, K. W. 14
Cresswell, J. W. 31
critical autoethnography
 definition of 35
 intersectionality 35–36
 performative body 35
 power relations 35
critical ethnography

definition of 28–31
ethnographic interview 28–31
power and inequality 28
positionality 32
reflexivity 31–32
subjectivity 32
critical intercultural communication 13–14
CIP (Critical Intercultural Performance) 14–16, 47–48, 66, 123
cultural reentry
definition of 77
home/host binary 77–79, 85, 123–124
short-term reentry 79–81, 85, 124
Cupach, W. R. 55, 83, 106, 124
cyberethnography
cyberspace 37–40, 124
definition of 37
ethnographic process 38–40
history of 37–38
other names for 37

definition of 54
ethnography
collection of data 27–28
critical approach to *see* critical ethnography
definition of 27–28

F

Fanon, F. 94
Featherstone, M. 11, 104
Fetterman, D. M. 39
Filipinization policies 49, 116
Filisino 51
Fischer, M. M. J. 28
Flaherty, M. G. 35
Flores, L. A. 60, 72, 93
Foley, D. 28

D

Dai, F. 118
Deitering, A. 36
diaspora
Chinese diaspora 9
critique of 7–9
definition of 7
Dippo, D. 28
Doeppers, D. F. 4
domestic workers 59
Douglas, K. 36
Drzewiecka, J. A. 7, 8, 83
Durham, M. G. 75
Dutta, M. 35

G

Gajjala, R. 8, 38–39, 92, 107, 124
Gama, E. 77
Garcia, A. C. 37, 38, 39
García Canclini, N. 10
Georgiou, M. 95
Ghabra, H. 15–16
G.I. (Genuine *Intsik*) 119–120
Gilroy, P. 8, 10, 100
Glesne, C. 29, 31
globalization 10–11, 52, 55–56, 80, 104
Goldschmidt, W. 34
Goltz, D. B. 31
Gomez, L. R. 72
Gómez-Peña, G. 10, 124
Gonzales, W. D. W. 4, 5
Gonzalez, A. 5
Gordon, N. S. 11, 56
Greenspan, H. 34
Greiner, C. 9
Griffin, R. A. 35
Guéguen, C. 6
Guillermo, A. R. 49, 51

E

Eguchi, S. 10, 14, 15, 31, 35, 78, 82, 83, 84, 85
Ellis, C. 33–35
ethnicity
ancestry 3, 5, 49–50, 54, 56, 63, 94–95

H

Hall, B. J. 13
Hall, S. 10, 57, 66, 81, 96, 100, 121
Halualani, R. T. 8, 10, 13, 15, 54, 55, 62, 81, 83
Hamera, J. 13, 14, 50, 53
Hammersley, M. 27, 31
Handelman, J. 39
Harvey, M. G. 77
Hasian, M. A. 93
Hau, C. S. 5, 119
Hayano, D. M. 34
Hegde, R. 10, 53, 56, 85
Heider, K. G. 34
Hobson, K. 14, 15
Hokkien
 as spoken language 5–6, 30–31, 40, 54, 64, 96–99, 117, 118, 122
 connection to Tsina/oy identity 50, 65, 80–81, 97–98, 103, 113–114
Holland, D. 28
Holman Jones, S. 34, 35
homeplace 26, 79
hooks, b. 8, 10, 26, 59, 79, 104
hybridity
 blending of cultures 10, 49–50, 64
 construction of subjectivities 10–11, 53, 64, 107
 in-between spaces 6, 10–11, 51, 55, 63–64, 81, 102, 104, 116, 125
 multiple tensions 6–7, 11–12, 61, 63–64, 66, 73, 75, 81, 84, 92, 102–103, 105–106, 124

I

Imahori, T. T. 55, 83, 106, 124
immigrant visas in the Philippines 118
institutional practices in the Philippines 113, 116–117
intersectionality
 definition of 14
 inclusion of (un)documented bodies 15, 32–33
 women and queer of color feminisms 14, 36
intsik 51, 59–60, 119

J

Jaworsky, B. N. 8, 9, 92
Johnson, A. L. 14
Jones Jr., R. G. 16, 32
Joseph, M. 11
Juan, G. B. 97

K

Kaisa para sa Kaunlaran 6, 48, 51
Kanno, Y. 85
Kendall, L. 37
Kibria, N. 86
Kim, Y. Y. 78
Kinchloe, L. J. 28
Kinefuchi, E. 79, 82
Klöter, H. 5
Knight, G. 54
Koike, K. 5
Kozinets, R. V. 39
Kraidy, M. M. 10, 11, 12, 49
Krizek, R. L. 16, 60

L

Lan, P. 59
Lane, J. 38
LeBesco, K. 38
Leeds-Hurwitz, W. 13, 103
Lema, K. 60
LeMaster, B. 14
Lester, J. N. 37, 38
Leung, L. 39
Levinson, B. A. 28
Levitt, P. 8, 9, 92

Lin, H. 15–16
Lionnet, F. 33, 34
Lum, C. M. K. 115
Lunar New Year 3, 6, 99–101, 105, 115

M

MacGowan, J. 30
Maclaran, P. 39
Madison, D. S. 13, 14, 28, 31, 32, 50, 53
Mandarin language 5–6, 54, 64, 93, 98–99, 116–117, 121–122
Marcos, F. 5, 76
Marcus, G. E. 28
Markham, A. N. 37, 38, 40
Martin, J. N. 13, 54, 58, 77, 78
matrix of domination 14
Mattson, M. 27, 28, 29, 30
McIntosh, D. M. D. 14, 15, 31, 74, 84
McLaren, P. 28, 31
Mendoza, S. L. 51, 55, 56
Meyerhoff, B. 31
Mid-Autumn Festival *see* Mooncake Festival
Miike, Y. 16
Minnan *see* Hokkien
Molina Guzmán, I. 10
Moon, D. G. 13, 14
Mooncake Festival 3, 6, 101
Moreman, S. T. 14
Murthy, D. 38

N

Naficy, H. 10
Nakayama, T. K. 13, 16, 54, 58, 60
Nam, V. 49
national identity
 definition of 54
 citizenship 14, 53–56, 82–83, 86, 103, 124
Noblit, G. W. 28
Nurse, K. 8

O

Oath of Allegiance
 history of 73–74
Ono, K. A. 13

P

Parreñas, R. S. 59
Pascual, M. R. 10, 11, 63, 103, 104
Pathak, A. 35
Pedersen, P. 77
Pensoneau-Conway, S. L. 33
performance studies 13–14, 123
performative act 50
Philippines, the
 Chinese mestiza/os in 3
 Chinese migrants in *see* Chinese in the Philippines
 Metro Manila area of 4–5, 57, 62
 official languages of 97
 Spanish colonization of 4–6, 51, 57, 62, 94, 115
 U.S. colonization of 5–6, 62, 94, 115, 119
Pinoy 3, 48, 51
Pinsino 51
positionality *see* critical ethnography
public pedagogies 116

Q

Quezon City 4, 118
Quezon, M. L. 5

R

Reed-Danahay, D. E. 35
reflexivity
 definition of 15, 16, 31, 32
 intersectional reflexivity 3, 16, 32, 40, 48, 123

INDEX

(trans)national hybrid reflexivity 15–16
Rivera, T. C. 5
Robinson, L. 37, 38, 39
Rogers, J. 77
Rohrlich, B. I. 77
Rosaldo, R. 14
Rowe, W. 102
Roy, C. 101
Rubin, H. J. 30
Rubin, I. S. 30
Rybas, N. 39

S

Safran, W. 7
Sakamoto, R. 65
Sakdapolrak, P. 9
Sandlin, J. A. 116
Sangleys 4, 51
Sarup, M. 86, 100, 107
Schelling, V. 102
Schulz, J. 37, 38, 39
See, S. B. O. 101
See, T. A. 3–4, 5, 6, 7, 9, 49, 50, 51, 53, 57, 62, 63, 64, 113, 115
Shi, Y. 7, 54, 85, 104
Shoham, A. 39
Shome, R. 12, 53, 56, 85
Shugart, H. A. 12
Simmel, G. 78
Simon, R. I. 28
Smith, S. 77
Spanish
  language in the Philippines 5–6
  colonization *see* the Philippines
Spieldenner, A. R. 35
Spradley, J. P. 29–30
Stage, C. W. 27, 28, 29, 30
Steyn, M. 83
Stone, A. R. 37
Sy, J. 4, 5

T

Tagalog
  national language 5, 117
  co-dominant language 5–6, 97
Taglish 2, 6, 26, 97
Tan, A. S. 5, 49, 52
Tan, C. 118
Tan, S. V. 4
Tankei-Aminian, S. 51
Taoism 6
TDK (*tai-diok-ka*) 119
Thomas, J. 28
Thomas, M. 94
Thompson, R. M. 5, 97
tiangge
  168 Shopping Mall 62, 117–118
  definition of 117
Tölölyan, K. 7
Tomlin, C. R. 77
Toyosaki, S. 33, 35
transnationalism
  definition of 8
  intersectionality 9
  justification for (trans)nationalism 9
Trinh, M. 35
Tsina/oys (Tsinoys)
  baby boomer 54, 113–114, 123
  meaning of 3, 48
  generational differences 3, 5–7, 50–51, 53, 64, 95, 103, 113–115, 117, 120–123
Turkle, S. 39
Turner, J. 38
Turner, V. W. 10

U

USCIS (United States Citizenship and Immigration Services) 71–73, 82, 125
Uytanlet, J. L. 4, 6, 48, 51, 59

V

Valdivia, A. N. 10
Van Maanen, J. 35
Vertovec, S. 7
Villenas, S. 28

W

Walstrom, M. K. 38
Ward, C. 77
Ward, K. 37

Warren, J. T. 13, 15, 31
Wenjing, X. 91
whiteness 12, 74, 84
Wickberg, E. 4
Wilson, A. H. 77

Y

Yap, J. P. 3, 48
Yep, G. A. 11, 14, 15, 53, 61, 82, 98, 102, 106, 107, 124
Young, S. L. 10, 11, 12, 49–50, 51, 85, 116
Yu, J. V. B. 6

Thomas K. Nakayama and Bernadette Marie Calafell, General Editors

Critical approaches to the study of intercultural communication have arisen at the end of the twentieth century and are poised to flourish in the new millennium. As cultures come into contact—driven by migration, refugees, the internet, wars, media, transnational capitalism, cultural imperialism, and more—critical interrogations of the ways that cultures interact communicatively are needed to understand culture and communication. This series will interrogate—from a critical perspective—the role of communication in intercultural contact, in both domestic and international contexts. This series is open to studies in key areas such as postcolonialism, transnationalism, critical race theory, queer diaspora studies, and critical feminist approaches as they relate to intercultural communication, tuning into the complexities of power relations in intercultural communication. Proposals might focus on various contexts of intercultural communication such as international advertising, popular culture, language policies, hate crimes, ethnic cleansing and ethnic group conflicts, as well as engaging theoretical issues such as hybridity, displacement, multiplicity, identity, orientalism, and materialism. By creating a space for these critical approaches, this series will be at the forefront of this new wave in intercultural communication scholarship. Manuscripts and proposals are welcome that advance this new approach.

For additional information about this series or for the submission of manuscripts, please contact:

Thomas K. Nakayama, General Editor | *T.Nakayama@neu.edu*
Bernadette Marie Calafell, General Editor | *calafell@gonzaga.edu*

To order other books in this series, please contact our Customer Service Department at:

peterlang@presswarehouse.com (within the U.S.)
orders@peterlang.com (outside the U.S.)

or browse online by series: www.peterlang.com

www.ingramcontent.com/pod-product-compliance
Lightning Source LLC
Chambersburg PA
CBHW061718300426
44115CB00014B/2740